The New Granville Island

Market Cookbook

The New Granville Island

Market Cookbook

Judie Glick and Carol Jensson

ARSENAL
PULP PRESS

THE NEW GRANVILLE ISLAND COOKBOOK
Copyright © 2012 by Judie Glick and Carol Jensson

All rights reserved. No part of this book may be reproduced
or used in any form by any means—graphic, electronic,
or mechanical—without the prior written permission of the
publisher, except by a reviewer, who may use brief excerpts
in a review, or in the case of photocopying in Canada,
a license from Access Copyright.

ARSENAL PULP PRESS
Suite 101, 211 East Georgia St.
Vancouver, BC
Canada V6A 1Z6
arsenalpulp.com

The publisher gratefully acknowledges the support of the
Government of Canada (through the Canada Book Fund)
and the Government of British Columbia (through the Book
Publishing Tax Credit Program) for its publishing activities.

The authors and publisher assert that the information contained
in this book is true and complete to the best of their knowledge.
All recommendations are made without guarantee on the part of
the author and publisher. The author and publisher disclaim any
liability with the use of this information. For more information,
contact the publisher.

Note to readers: some ingredients are measured by volume
(i.e., cups and millilitres), not weight.

Book design by Lisa Eng-Lodge, Electra Design Group
Photography by Tracey Kusiewicz
Food styling by Carol Jensson

Printed and bound in China

Library and Archives Canada Cataloguing in Publication

Glick, Judie, 1944-

    The new Granville Island Market cookbook / Judie Glick and Carol
Jensson.

Includes index.

Issued also in an electronic format.

ISBN 978-1-55152-439-9

    1. Cooking, Canadian. 2. Local foods--Canada. 3. Granville Island
(Vancouver, B.C.) 4. Cookbooks I. Jensson, Carol II. Title.

TX715.6.G615 2012   641.59711'33   C2011-908405-8

Contents

Introduction

When we started our businesses in the Granville Island Public Market in 1979, the changes that were about to shake up the world of food and cooking in the 1980s were yet to begin.

Foodies were just starting to discover little known but exciting fruits and vegetables—kiwis from New Zealand, lychee and mangosteen from Asia, and countless others.

While the Public Market was known in Vancouver as a fresh food market rather than a farmer's market—farmers displayed their wares on "day tables"—it was the permanent shops selling fresh fish, produce, and other goods that brought everyone to the Market from the start. Okanagan fruit, from British Columbia's Interior, could be bought without going to the Okanagan, fresh bagels were made on site, and there was an espresso bar with a beautiful view of the water (False Creek). It was a new place in a new part of town. And what a setting!

Sunday shopping was a rarity in Vancouver in the 1980s, but because Granville Island is on federally owned land, we could be open on Sundays. The Market was accessible: people could come from downtown by boat, parking was free, a public transit bus came right to the Island. Shopping at the Market on Sundays became a weekly ritual for many Vancouverites. Throughout the 1970s and '80s, the land at nearby False Creek was developed, and more people moved there. Here was a new community that offered mixed housing, an elementary school, a community centre and, in 1979, the Public Market. It became a village within the city.

The Market continues to be a vibrant place known for fresh, local, quality food. What's changed in the last thirty years is the way food is talked about; the vocabulary of food. It's no longer discussed only among farmers or in women's magazines. One influential personality was local chef James Barber (1923–2007), who taped more than 500 episodes

of his TV program *The Urban Peasant*, which broadcast throughout North America in the 1980s. Carol worked with James on the set and recalls that he wanted, above all, to demystify cooking. The motto of the show was "Do the best you can with what you've got," even if a recipe called for wine and you had only apple juice.

By the early '90s, cooking shows on the Food Network and elsewhere produced celebrity chefs, and the vocabulary of food changed again. Soon food shows became competitive and challenging with programs like *Iron Chef*, *Top Chef*, and Gordon Ramsey's *Hell's Kitchen*. Today, food trends now spread instantly through social media, and food newsletters have become food blogs. Culinary schools have opened in cities around the world (as culinary tourism became a trend), and now it seems like everyone is taking cooking classes. Vancouver's Barbara-Jo's Books to Cooks, for example, sells not only books, but hosts classes and dinners based on recipe books—cooking is seen as an evening's entertainment.

In the last decade, we've also become more concerned about where our food comes from and how it is grown. Environmental and health concerns have emphasized the need for more local and organic food, and the benefits of supporting farmer's markets. So the vocabulary of food continues to change. We are deepening our knowledge of what we are buying and seeking closer relationships with the people who produce our food.

The Public Market on Granville Island continues the tradition of supplying fresh, local products that evolve with time: as we write, a new day table is selling vegan treats.

Come listen to our stories, try some new recipes, and rediscover old gems. Read, shop, cook, and eat. Repeat until well seasoned.

—Judie Glick and Carol Jensson

Fall

The rhythm of the Market takes on a less hectic pace when summer's over, but for some merchants this is the busiest time. After Labour Day, older tourists (without school-age children) visit the Market, students come in after school, and local chefs are again seen strolling the Market after their summer apprentices have left. When the last of the local harvest arrives, devoted jam-makers and "preservationists" come to buy the berries, fruits, and vegetables that won't be available until next year. Cucumbers, apples, and squash are in their prime now, and it's time to eat, can, and freeze, knowing that fresh produce from local farms is always the best bet for quality. Specialty apple growers from Vancouver Island present their goods on the day tables. Pumpkins bring an orange hue to produce stands.

In the fall, making soup seems like a good idea again, and if meat had a season, fall would be it: a roast beef dinner with root vegetables and gravy has a certain appeal, especially when there is a chill in the air. As the days shorten, the warm glow of lights inside the Market show off the merchants' displays. So, even though the good weather and tourist season has disappeared for another year, the Market continues to thrive by offering the fruits of fall harvests.

Appetizers & Snacks

Mushroom-Stuffed Puff Pastry

This savoury appetizer can be made either as a single large rectangle and then cut into individual portions or used to fill vol-au-vent shells. Either way, it's delicious!

1 tbsp	butter
1 tbsp	extra virgin olive oil
1	medium onion, finely chopped
1 lb	(500 g) fresh wild or cultivated mushrooms, washed and trimmed
¼ cup	(60 mL) white wine or sherry
1 tbsp	fresh thyme leaves
1 large	sheet puff pastry, 12 x 12 in (30 x 30 cm), thawed (or 8 pre-made frozen vol-au-vent shells)
1 large	egg, beaten

Preheat oven to 400°F (200°C).

In a large heavy frying pan on medium heat, melt butter with the oil. Add the onion and sauté for 2 minutes. Add the mushrooms, wine, and thyme and sauté until the liquid has evaporated. Remove from heat and cool to room temperature.

Place the puff pastry on a parchment-lined baking sheet and lay the mushroom mixture on top, leaving a 2-in (5-cm) border around the edges. Fold over the pastry 1 in (2.5 cm) from the edges, then fold up to create a ridge around the filling. Brush the border with the beaten egg. (If using vol-a-vent shells, put 3 tbsp filling in each.) Place the sheet on middle rack in oven and bake until the pastry is golden and puffed, about 20 minutes. Cool for 5 minutes before serving.

Makes 12 slices or 8 vols-au-vent.

Skinny Onion Pie

Onions are one of our favourite vegetables—such variety, so much taste, they can be enjoyed alone or with almost anything. Reasonably priced, most often grown locally, onions rule in cooking. And most people can grow some kind of onion, even in a pot. Judie has a travelling onion that sets its own seeds, providing an endless source of green onion stems.

This pie recipe uses less cream and cheese than many others—hence the "skinny"!

6 tbsp	unsalted butter
2–3 oz	(60–90 g) crackers (about 20 "saltine"-style)
4½ cups	(590 g) thinly sliced cooking onions
½ tsp	kosher salt
2	eggs
¾ cup	(185 mL) heavy cream (or milk)
3 oz	(90 g) grated Emmental or Parmesan cheese

Preheat oven to 375°F (190°C).

In a large skillet or sauté pan on low heat melt 3 tbsp butter. Set aside.

Crumble the crackers to a fine crumb in a medium bowl. Pour melted butter over crumbs and toss with fingertips until evenly coated. Press mixture firmly into a deep-dish 9-in (23-cm) pie plate, using a second plate, if possible, to compact it evenly against bottom and sides of pan.

Melt the remaining butter in skillet on medium-high heat until frothy. Add the onions and ¼ tsp salt. Cook, stirring constantly, until onions are evenly browned, 15–20 minutes.

Transfer onions to the pie plate, patting them down in an even layer on the crust. In a medium bowl, beat the eggs, and add cream or milk and remaining salt, whisking gently to incorporate. Pour mixture slowly, in a thin stream, into the centre of the onions in the pie pan. Sprinkle grated cheese on top and place in oven. Bake until puffy and slightly browned on top, 30–35 minutes. Cool to room temperature. Slice with a serrated knife and serve.

Makes 3–4 servings as an appetizer.

Fiona's Antipasto

Another keeper from the first edition, this ambitious recipe is well worth the effort. Judie's first co-author, Fiona McLeod, is a purist about hand-chopping the ingredients, but those of you so inclined might want to use your food processor for this one. The original recipe was the work of two people over a weekend of fun and preserving. We've cut back the amounts by one half to make a smaller yield.

1 lb	(500 g) cauliflower, cut into bite-sized florets
1 lb	(500 g) green beans, trimmed and cut into bite-sized pieces
¾ lb	(375 g) young thin carrots, scrubbed and cut into bite-sized diagonal pieces
1 lb	(500 g) green bell peppers, cored and chopped
1 lb	(500 kg) red bell peppers, cored and chopped
1 lb	(500 g) small silverskin onions, peeled (for an easier peel, soak in cold water first)
½ tbsp	extra virgin olive oil
12 cups	(2.8 L) classic tomato sauce (p. 70)
2 6-oz	(178-mL) cans solid white tuna, with oil
½ 7-oz	(250-g) can anchovies
8 cups	(1–1.5 kg) black olives, pitted
4 cups	(720 g) green olives, pitted
1 lb	(500 g) mushrooms, sliced
2½ cups	(600 mL) marinated artichoke hearts, with oil

In a large pot, blanch the cauliflower, beans, and carrots until tender-crisp, about 5 minutes in boiling water. Hard vegetables should just start to feel soft to a fork. Refresh in cold water. In a large frying pan, sauté the peppers and onions in olive oil until just softened. Place vegetables, with the cooking liquids, into a large pot. Add tomato sauce, tuna, and anchovies. Bring to a boil, then add the rest of ingredients and cook for 5 minutes.

Put hot antipasto into sterilized pint jars and process in a hot water-bath canner for 15 minutes.

Makes 15 pints (7 L).

Kim Chi

This spicy Korean condiment is a wonderful accompaniment to soups, stir fries, and many rice dishes. Sambal Olek is an Indonesian hot sauce available at Asian market.

2 heads	napa cabbage
½ cup	(125 mL) salt
2 tbsp	fish sauce
4	green onions, finely chopped
2	garlic cloves, minced
2 tbsp	white sugar
1 tbsp	fresh ginger, minced
4 tbsp	Korean hot sauce, Sambal Olek, or any Chinese chili paste

Cut the cabbage into 2-in (5-cm) wedges. Dissolve salt in a large bowl with 4 cups (1 L) water. Soak the cabbage in the salty water for 3–4 hours. Rinse off and drain the cabbage well.

In a large bowl, combine the rest of the ingredients and add the cabbage, mixing it well to coat all the leaves. Transfer to a large container and refrigerate for 2–3 days so that the flavours can marry. Then store in a glass container in refrigerator for up to 1 month.

Makes about 12 cups (2.8 L).

Mango Chutney

This recipe is from our dear friend and chef extraordinaire Evonne Karie. Evonne worked, shopped at, and promoted the Market when she lived in Vancouver.

4	large ripe mangoes, peeled, seeded, and cut into small pieces
1	small red pepper, diced
1	medium onion, finely chopped
1½ cups	(375 mL) brown sugar
½ cup	(125 mL) white wine vinegar
¼ cup	(60 mL) grated fresh ginger
2 tsp	curry powder
2 tbsp	freshly squeezed lemon juice
½ tsp	cinnamon
½ tsp	nutmeg

Place all the ingredients in a stainless steel pan on medium heat and let simmer for 45 minutes to 1 hour. Once all the ingredients are blended and cooked, place the hot chutney into self-sealing jars or use a traditional hot water-bath method and process in boiling water for 10 minutes.

Makes 6 cups (1.4 L).

One of Evonne's favourite dips is made by adding ¼ cup (60 mL) cooked mango chutney to 1 cup (250 mL) mayonnaise. Add 2 tsp fresh lemon juice and 1 tsp curry powder and blend in food processor. This makes a lovely aioli dip for crudités.

Soups & Salads

Butternut Squash Soup

Perfect as a first course, we've adapted this classic recipe to make a lighter alternative to the traditional creamier version—and it's just as delicious.

2 tbsp	extra virgin olive oil
1	small onion, chopped
2	stalks celery, chopped
1	medium carrot, chopped
1	medium butternut squash, peeled, seeded, and cubed
3 cups	(750 mL) chicken or vegetable stock
1 cup	(250 mL) apple juice
	salt and freshly ground pepper, to taste

In a large saucepan on medium, heat the olive oil for about 1 minute. Add the onions, celery, carrots, and squash and cook until lightly browned. Pour in enough stock (approx. 2 cups [500 mL]) to cover the vegetables and bring to a boil. Reduce the heat and simmer until the vegetables are tender. Let cool slightly, transfer the soup to a blender or food processor (you can also use a hand blender in the pot), and blend until smooth (be careful when blending hot liquids). Return the soup to the pot, add the rest of the stock, apple juice, salt, and pepper and bring to a simmer until warm.

Makes 4 servings.

Beet and Goat Cheese Pasta Salad

Cold pasta salads came into their own in the '80s. Old-school Italian cooks were mystified: "You eat noodles cold?" But everyone else loved them. Salads have moved from being side dishes to meals unto themselves. Add pasta to the beet and goat cheese salad we know and love for a full-meal deal. Balsamic reduction is a bottled product found in better grocery stores.

½ lb	(250 g) dried fussili
1 lb	(500 g) red beets cut in half, if large
¼ cup	(60 mL) red wine vinegar
4 tbsp	lemon juice
2	garlic cloves, crushed
4 tbsp	fresh dill
1	dried chili pepper, crumbled
6 tbsp	extra virgin olive oil
2 tbsp	balsamic reduction (syrup)
½ tsp	Dijon-style mustard
3½ oz	(100 g) goat cheese

In a large pot, cook the pasta in boiling salted water. Add the beets and cook until tender. Drain and set aside. When beets have cooled, peel and cut into 1-inch cubes and return to pasta. In a small bowl, combine the vinegar, 2 tbsp lemon juice, 1 crushed garlic clove, 2 tbsp dill, and chili pepper and pour over the warm pasta and beets. Set aside to cool.

In a small bowl, combine the rest of ingredients. Pour over pasta and beets and mix well. Crumble goat cheese on top and serve.

Makes 4 main or 8 side servings.

Vegetables

Artichoke Hash

This dish can be eaten hot or cold, but it is best when made in advance and reheated.

8 small	artichokes (or 4 medium or 2 large)		¼ cup	(60 mL) extra virgin olive oil
1 cup	(250 mL) diced carrots		2 tbsp	tomato paste or sundried tomato pesto
½ cup	(125 mL) diced celery			
1 medium	onion, diced		3 cups	(750 mL) water or seasoned broth
2	garlic cloves, coarsely chopped			
1½ cups	(375 mL) diced Yukon Gold potatoes			

Prepare the artichokes as described in sidebar. Cut large ones in half. Let sit in acidulated water (2 tbsp lemon juice or vinegar to 4 cups [1 L] water) until ready to cook to prevent discolouration.

In a large saucepan, sauté the diced vegetables, garlic and potatoes in oil until onions are golden. Watch that potatoes don't stick. Stir tomato paste into the water and pour over vegetables. Place artichokes in saucepan, cover, and simmer until tender, about 25 minutes. The artichokes are done when they are soft enough to be pierced by a fork. (If using baby or small artichokes, you can cook these on top of the vegetable hash, which gives it that great artichoke flavour.)

Makes 4 servings.

Artichokes

John and Donna Plough of Glen Valley Artichoke Farms in the Fraser Valley started growing artichokes in the '90s and have been selling them on Thursdays at the Market ever since. (See Donna's apple pie recipe, p. 48.)

Artichokes should be judged by the shape of their buds and their tightness, not size. Wash them thoroughly by soaking in water for 5–10 minutes, then drain. If they are large, slice 1 in (2.5 cm) off the thorny tops with a large knife and trim the thorny lower leaves with scissors. Remove the purple leaves and "hairs" (the choke) from the centre. If the stem is tough, remove; otherwise peel and trim. Artichokes can be cut in half for smaller portions or faster cooking.

Puttanesca Sauce

This dish from the south of Italy exemplifies the beauty of simple pasta sauces from this region. Serve with your favourite pasta and a green side salad for a perfect fall weekend supper.

2 tbsp	extra virgin olive oil
1 medium	onion, finely chopped
3	garlic cloves, finely chopped
1 14-oz	(398-mL) can whole plum tomatoes
2 tbsp	capers, drained
½ cup	(125 mL) Kalamata olives, pitted and quartered
1 tsp	dried oregano
1 tsp	chili flakes
	salt and freshly ground pepper, to taste
6	anchovy filets, mashed, or 1 tbsp anchovy paste (optional)
2 tbsp	fresh parsley, finely chopped

In a large heavy-bottomed skillet on medium, heat the olive oil. Sauté the onions and garlic until soft. Add the rest of the ingredients, except the parsley, and simmer for 10 minutes. Add the parsley just before serving.

Makes about 3 cups (750 mL).

Mashed Potatoes with Shallots

This dish is a real winner at dinner parties. The shallots give the potatoes a beautiful mahogany colour and they taste as good as they look.

2 lb	(1 kg) Yukon Gold potatoes, peeled and quartered
2 tbsp	butter
1½ cups	(375 mL) shallots, peeled and sliced
¾ cup	(185 mL) milk
4 tbsp	butter
	salt and freshly ground pepper, to taste

In a large saucepan, add enough cold water to completely cover the potatoes by 1 in (2.5 cm). Bring to a boil and reduce heat to medium. Cook for about 20 minutes, until the potatoes are tender.

While potatoes are cooking, melt 2 tbsp butter in a heavy skillet on medium heat. Add the shallots and sauté until brown and tender, about 15 minutes. Drain the potatoes and return to the pot. Add the milk, 4 tbsp butter, salt and pepper, and mash well. Stir in shallots with a wooden spoon and serve.

Makes 6 servings.

Grazyna Martusewicz and B.J. Rodgers from La Tortilleria.

Tortillas Chilaquiles

Another great recipe from the first edition of our cookbook, this vegetarian dish uses up leftover tortillas. The Market tradition of Mexican food is carried on by Betty Rodgers and Grazyna Martusewicz of La Tortilleria, who work in what is probably the smallest space in the Market, selling tortillas, rice and beans, tacos, burritos, guacamole, and much more. Mexican-style beans are the perfect accompaniment to this hearty and easy-to-make main dish.

½ cup	(125 mL) canola oil
12	corn tortillas, cut into quarters
6	large tomatoes
1 medium	onion, finely chopped
2	garlic cloves, minced
1 tsp	salt
2–3	jalapeño peppers, finely chopped*
3 large	sprigs fresh cilantro, chopped
2½ cups	(625 mL) Monterey cheese, grated

Preheat oven to 350°F (180°C).

In a heavy skillet on medium, heat the oil. Fry the tortillas until golden but not crisp. Drain on paper towels. Leave the oil in the pan for the sauce.

In a blender or food processor, purée the tomatoes, onions, garlic, salt, peppers, and cilantro. Add the mixture to the skillet and cook for about 5 minutes. In a greased baking dish, place one layer of tortillas and cover with half the tomato sauce. Top with half the cheese. Repeat. Bake 30 minutes.

Makes 4 servings.

* **Note:** *Wear latex gloves to scrape out spicy jalapeño pepper seeds with a knife blade; be careful not to get them on your bare hands or to touch your face with your gloved hands—these seeds can burn!*

Cauliflower, Chickpea, and Kale Curry

This vegetarian recipe comes from our multi-talented photographer and friend Tracey Kusiewicz. Serve on brown rice and top with finely diced green apple, fresh cilantro, and chopped almonds.

2 tbsp	sesame oil
3 cups	(750 mL) cauliflower, cut into small florets
1 tbsp	finely chopped lemongrass
1 tbsp	finely chopped fresh ginger
2 tbsp	curry powder
	salt, to taste
1 tbsp	finely chopped fresh garlic
¾ cup	(175 mL) diced leeks
1 14-oz	(398-mL) can coconut milk
1 bunch	curly kale (about 2 cups/500 mL), stalks removed and finely chopped
1 19-oz	(540-mL) can chickpeas
1 tbsp	fresh lime juice

SUGGESTED GARNISHES:

2 tsp	chopped fresh cilantro
2 tbsp	chopped almonds
2 tbsp	finely diced green apple

In a large frying pan on medium, heat the sesame oil. Add the cauliflower, lemongrass, ginger, curry powder, and salt. Sauté for 3–5 minutes. Reduce heat to medium-low, add garlic, leeks, and ¾ of the can of coconut milk, and simmer for another 10 minutes, until cauliflower is al dente. Add the kale, chickpeas, and remaining coconut milk and continue to simmer for another 5 minutes, until the coconut milk is reduced. Add lime juice, garnish as desired, and serve.

Makes 4 servings.

Entrées

Breakfast Casserole

There are many versions of this dish, but we like this one best. Make it easy on yourself and prepare the ingredients the night before and then bake it in the morning. We like to use croissants or challah (egg-based bread) for more richness. You can add any little extras (like mushrooms, peppers, tomatoes, or fresh herbs) to spice it up or use veggie sausage or ham. It's yummy served with homemade chutney (p. 20).

2 cups	(500 mL) stale bread torn into chunks
1 cup	(250 mL) grated Cheddar cheese
1 cup	(250 mL) cooked sausage meat
8	eggs
2 cups	(500 mL) milk or cream
2 tsp	dry mustard
1 tsp	salt
	freshly ground pepper, to taste

Preheat oven to 350°F (180°C).

Grease a 9 x 13-in (22 x 33-cm) glass baking dish. Place the bread in the dish. Top the bread with cheese and sausage. Beat together the eggs, milk, mustard, salt, and pepper. Pour the egg mixture over all.

Chill overnight or for at least 1 hour. Bake until the centre is set and the casserole is puffy, about 45 minutes.

Makes 6 servings.

Turkey Meatballs

These are a tasty, low-fat alternative to beef meatballs. We serve them with pasta and tomato sauce (p. 70) or flatten them into patties before baking to make turkey "sliders."

1 lb	(500 g) lean ground turkey
1 tbsp	Dijon mustard
1 tbsp	Worcestershire sauce
2 tsp	dried dill weed
2 tsp	dried oregano
1 tsp	onion powder
1 tsp	garlic powder
1 tsp	seasoned salt
	freshly ground pepper, to taste
	1–2 drops of your favourite hot sauce (optional)

Preheat oven to 350°F (180°C).

Place all the ingredients in a large bowl. Mix well—your hands are best for this—and form into golf ball-sized balls. (Now's the time to flatten them into little patties if you are making sliders.) Place the meatballs on a cookie sheet lined with foil or parchment and bake for about 20–25 minutes, turning over half way through the cooking time. Don't overcook them, or they will be dry.

Makes 12–15 meatballs.

Turducken for Two

Many cooks will remember the "turducken" from the late '80s when it was first introduced as a southern US specialty dish which involved stuffing a de-boned duck into a de-boned chicken, then into a de-boned turkey, sometimes with stuffing (dressing) between the birds. This was great for TV, but something rarely done at home or even in restaurants. A few specialty butchers still prepare turducken to order. The big deal is in the presentation and ease of carving: sliced turducken looks like a very fancy meat loaf.

The idea of stuffing small game into bigger game dates back to the Roman Empire. The French word for stuffing, farce, *is often used to refer to this practice, as was the early nineteenth-century feast made from more than a dozen stuffed fowl,* rôti sans pareil *(roast without equal).*

This recipe makes a nod to all the above, but is more simple and delicious. By making the stuffing a day in advance, you can save time for the main event. (P.S. The stuffing is great for any bird.)

STUFFING:

½ lb	(250 g) chicken giblets (heart and liver)
6 oz	(175 g) Italian sausage with fennel seeds
2 tbsp	cooking oil
¼ tsp	fennel seeds
⅓ cup	(80 mL) diced carrots
¼ cup	(60 mL) diced celery
¼ cup	(60 mL) diced onion
¼ cup	(40 mL) brandy
¼ tsp	dried thyme
¼ tsp	dried tarragon
	salt and pepper, to taste
1½ cups	(375 mL) good white bread (not sourdough), torn into bite-sized pieces

Preheat oven to 350°F (180°C).

In a pot of water, boil the giblets until cooked thoroughly, about 15 minutes. Let cool, then chop and set aside. Remove casings from sausages and in a frying pan on medium heat, sauté the sausages in oil with the fennel seeds. Add the carrots, celery, and onions. Stir in giblets. Sauté until mixed but not overcooked. Stir in the brandy. Add the dried herbs, salt, and pepper. Adjust amounts of fennel seeds and brandy to your taste.

Place the bread pieces in a large bowl. Combine with the sausage mixture, using your hands. Set aside and prepare the turducken.

TURDUCKEN:

1 6–8 oz   (175–230 g) boneless turkey thigh, with skin on
              salt for seasoning
1 3–4 oz   (90–115 g) boneless, skinless chicken breast
      1   boneless duck breast, skin on (note: Muscovy duck breasts are bigger and more available and should be cut in half. Pekin duck breasts are smaller and may require 2 portions)

If your turducken is too thick, it can dry out when baked. It is hard to get both turkey thighs and chicken breasts in uniform sizes or thickness. This recipe works best when they are thin and small.

Place the turkey thigh, skin side down, in a small roasting pan that can be covered. Salt lightly and spread half the stuffing over top. Add the chicken breast. Spread the rest of the stuffing on top of the chicken. Add the duck breast on top, skin side up. Wrap the roast in cheesecloth to keep it together while in the oven. Place in a covered roasting pan and roast for 1 hour. Check and baste every 15 minutes. Duck breast should be well browned. Remove cheesecloth before serving.

Makes 2 servings.

Foodie, PhD

Since we started working at the Market, we've seen the food industry grow and offer a multitude of career choices for people interested in the culinary arts, from restaurant or personal chef to caterer for individuals, groups, or institutions, from beverage manager to food writer—there are even food studies programs in universities, something we could not have imagined when we started our careers as foodies.

Lentils with Duck Confit

As people who like to cook and eat, we're open to any tips or tricks available that will get dinner on the table without too much effort. Cassoulet is traditionally made with beans, sausages, and ham. You can make it with lentils for a quicker, leaner, easier meal that will still taste like the French version. Pre-cooked duck confit (salt-cured duck poached in its own fat) is available at Oyama Sausage Company at the Granville Island Market and from your local quality butcher shop. Add your favourite sausage to this dish if you have big eaters at your dinner table. This recipe is from Lucy Waverman, Food Columnist, The Globe and Mail, with thanks.

1 tbsp	extra virgin olive oil		4 cups	(1 L) chicken stock or water
1 cup	(250 mL) chopped onions		4 pieces	duck confit legs
½ cup	(125 mL) chopped celery		6 cups	(230 g) baby spinach
1 tsp	chopped garlic		3 tbsp	balsamic vinegar
1½ cup	(375 mL) green lentils			salt and freshly ground pepper, to taste
1	bay leaf			
4	thyme sprigs		2 tbsp	chopped fresh parsley

Preheat oven to 400°F (200°C).

In a pot on medium, heat the oil. Add the onions, celery, and garlic and sauté until softened, about 2–3 minutes. Add lentils and sauté for 1 minute. Add bay leaf, thyme, and stock and bring to boil. Reduce heat, cover, and simmer until lentils are cooked, about 35–40 minutes. Uncover pot for last 5 minutes, stirring occasionally. Drain off excess liquid. Discard thyme sprigs and bay leaf and reserve lentils.

While lentils are cooking, heat a large non-stick, ovenproof skillet on medium-high. Add the duck confit legs, skin-side down, and cook for 2 minutes or until brown and starting to crisp. Turn legs over, place skillet in oven, and bake for 10–15 minutes or until duck is hot and skin is crisp. Remove duck from pan. (*Tip:* Cover burning-hot skillet handle with an oven glove while finishing dish.) Add the spinach to the duck fat in the pan and sauté for 1 minute or until wilted. Add the reserved lentils and vinegar and cook, stirring, for 3 minutes or until hot. Season well with salt and pepper. Place lentils on a plate and top with duck confit. Sprinkle with parsley.

Makes 4 servings.

Oven-Fried Parmesan Chicken

From the original edition, this crispy chicken is good hot or cold. Serve with Mashed Potatoes with Shallots (p. 28) and some steamed greens for a great comfort-food supper.

3 lb	(1 kg) chicken pieces (legs, thighs, breasts)
1 cup	(250 mL) milk
12	crackers, crushed to fine crumbs—any kind (remember that flavoured crackers, such as garlic or herb, will add that taste to the chicken)
¼ cup	(60 mL) freshly grated Parmesan cheese
2 tbsp	parsley, finely chopped
1 tbsp	freshly ground black pepper
1 tsp	salt
2 tbsp	canola oil

Preheat oven to 450°F (230°C).

Place the chicken pieces in a shallow bowl and cover with the milk. Set aside.
Place the crushed crackers, Parmesan cheese, parsley, pepper, and salt into a plastic bag. Shake the excess milk off the chicken and place, one piece at a time, into the bag. Shake well to coat the chicken.

Lay the coated chicken pieces on a lightly oiled baking sheet. Drizzle the oil over the chicken, and bake for 30–45 minutes.

Makes 4 servings.

Pot Roast with Red Wine

Here's a basic recipe for a traditional dinner on a cool fall evening. There are many opinions on the best cut of beef for this dish; chuck, brisket, and bottom or top rounds are commonly used.

3–4 lb	(1.5–1.8 kg) beef roast
2 tsp	salt or seasoned salt
2 tsp	freshly ground pepper
2 tbsp	canola oil
1 large	onion, coarsely chopped
4	garlic cloves, peeled and halved
¾ cup	(185 mL) red wine

Preheat oven to 325°F (160°C).

Rub the salt and pepper onto the outside of the roast. In a large Dutch oven or roasting pan on high, heat the oil for 1 minute. Brown the roast on all sides. Add the onions and garlic to the pan and pour the red wine over it. Cover and place in the oven for about 3 hours.

Makes 10 servings.

Meat at the Market

When the Oyama Sausage Company deli opened in the Market many years ago, customer lineups were large from the start.

Offering free food samples and having knowledgeable staff helped to make them a huge success. The boring "cold cuts" of the past became gourmet charcuterie, and Oyama's delectable seasonal menus brought out the meat-eater in everyone.

By the early '90s, cuts of meat and chicken, already seasoned and sometimes sauced, became available at the two Market butcher shops. But as Vancouver journalist and bestselling novelist Timothy Taylor wrote in the *Globe and Mail*, butcher shop customers hadn't yet caught up to the geekiness that obsessed coffee drinkers and vegetarians.

"I tend to think the lag in butcher shops catching up to this vibe is because we still consume meat with a trace of guilty conscience. It's an aesthetic thing, partly. There's flesh and blood involved. But maybe another part of it is cultural, as gloomy environmental news encourages us to second guess our moral ranking in the food chain."

With the growing popularity of television food shows, customers started to talk about different cuts of meat—what to look for and where it came from. Taylor said: "At these shops you will find lots of chat back and forth between customers and staff on the topic at hand, meat ... The expertise is assumed, and the quality improves immediately."

So let's thank our modern-day butchers and sausage purveyors, the experts who know their meat!

Marinated Rib-Eye Steak

Keep the barbecue humming through the fall and enjoy this quick and easy recipe.

½ cup	(125 mL) balsamic vinegar
¼ cup	(60 mL) soy sauce
3 tbsp	minced garlic
2 tbsp	extra virgin olive oil
2 tbsp	brown sugar
1 tsp	Worcestershire sauce
1 tbsp	black pepper
1 tsp	salt
2½-lb	(250-g) rib-eye steaks

Preheat grill to medium-high.

In a shallow glass dish, combine all the ingredients (except the steaks) to make marinade. Place the steaks in the marinade and turn to coat. Refrigerate for 2 hours or up to overnight. Remove from refrigerator, discard the marinade, and let the steaks stand at room temperature for 1 hour. Grill the steaks 4–5 minutes on each side or to desired doneness.

Makes 2 servings.

Mike Suleman from Tenderland Meats.

Grilling meat

While writing the new edition of this cookbook, we realized that though ingredients and recipes may change over time, know-how and experience still pay off in the end.

In that spirit, here are some tried-and-true grilling tips.

• Thin cuts of meat will seldom yield that moist, tender interior and crisp browned exterior that are the barbecuer's ideal. Buy thicker cuts and slice them before serving.

• Let the meat sit at room temperature for at least 1 hour before grilling.

• Don't salt the meat before you cook it. Salt draws out moisture quickly and can make the meat tough. For skewer cooking, choose items that will cook at the same rate: put meat on one skewer, vegetables on another.

• The French use the term *à point,* medium rare, to describe the cooking stage at which meat begins to "sweat." When tiny pink droplets form on the surface of the meat, it means it is medium rare. As the surface begins to dry, the meat rapidly becomes well done.

• A room-temperature, 1¼-inch (3-cm) thick steak will be *à point* after about 4 minutes on one side and 4–5 minutes on the second side. It's a good idea to time this when you are first learning the technique.

• Let cooked meat sit for 10–15 minutes before slicing to retain its juices.

Fruits, Sweets, & Baked Goo

Donna's Apple Pie

The Thursday Truck Farmer's Market has been a summer event at Granville Island for a number of years. It's a relaxed affair and has grown to take up more space in Triangle Square outside the Market. Known as the "artichoke lady," Donna Plough is a long-time regular who offers loads of fresh produce and some canned items from her farm in Abbotsford.

Last year at the Market's first annual pie contest, Donna won bragging rights for hers, which she called "Grandma's Stolen Apple Pie." Donna and Judie agreed to a trade: Judie gave her the artichoke hash recipe (p. 26) in exchange for this, her winning pie recipe.

1 cup	(250 mL) sugar
1 tsp	cinnamon
½ tsp	nutmeg
2 portions	pie dough (opposite page)
¼ cup	flour, for rolling out dough
5–7	Gravenstein or Granny Smith apples (exact amount depends on the size of the pie plate)

Preheat oven to 400°F (250°C).

Mix sugar, cinnamon, and nutmeg in a bowl and set aside.

Form one ball of dough into a disk shape with your hands. Spread the flour onto a counter or cutting board. Roll out dough until large enough to drape over the edge of your pie plate. Put the dough into the pie plate: first, loosen the dough from the counter, then roll it back onto the rolling pin, and unroll over plate. Gently press into place. Sprinkle a bit of the spice/sugar mixture into the bottom of the shell. (With any leftover dough, make a jam or apple turnover for that special someone.)

Peel and thinly slice the apples. Arrange a single layer of apples, sprinkle with more sugar/spice mixture, and repeat, ending with sugar/spice mixture. Prepare the second ball of dough and roll out the top pie shell to cover the apples completely. Press down lightly and pinch the edges together. Cut off excess dough from around the edge of the pie plate. Make stem vent holes in the top shell.

Place in oven and bake for 15 minutes. Reduce heat to 350°F (180°C) and bake for 30–35 minutes, until the juices bubble through the crust. Cool for 20 minutes.

Makes 1 pie.

A.J.'s Pie Crust Dough

From the original book, Auntie Jessie was Judie's neighbour in Fort Langley. This is an old-style pie crust, easy to freeze, so that it is handy when needed.

4 cups	(1 L) flour
½ tsp	salt
1 lb	(500 g) margarine
1 cup	(250 mL) sour cream

Mix the flour and salt together in a large bowl. Add the margarine and sour cream and blend quickly with your fingers. Form into one large ball, then divide into it into four equal sections. Shape each section into a ball and wrap separately in wax paper. Freeze in plastic bags.

Makes 4 portions.

Apples

Fruit trees take a long time to grow. A farmer once told me that you don't want to be an old farmer with old trees that need to be replaced: planting new varieties takes time and energy and years for new trees to bear fruit.

Back in the late '70s, available apple varieties were limited: Red and Golden Delicious, Spartan, and very few others. It took a long time for the Galas, Granny Smiths, and the wonderful late apples—McIntoshes, Jonamacs, and Cortlands—we now enjoy to get into production. Thank you, apple orchardists, young and old, for taking us into the future.

Apple Crisp

This is a perfect and easy-to-make fall dessert, delicious with vanilla ice cream.

5 large	local, seasonal apples, peeled, cored, and sliced
3 tbsp	flour
½ cup	(125 mL) brown sugar
2 tbsp	maple syrup
1 tbsp	lemon juice
1 tsp	lemon zest

TOPPING:

1 cup	(250 mL) all purpose flour
1 cup	(250 mL) brown sugar
1 cup	(250 mL) oats
½ cup	(125 mL) butter, melted
2 tsp	cinnamon
1 tsp	cardamom

Preheat oven to 400°F (200°C).

In a medium bowl, mix the apples, flour, brown sugar, syrup, lemon juice, and zest until well blended. Place the apple mixture into a greased 9 x 13-in (23 x 33-cm) baking dish. (Or, for individual portions, use 4 1-cup [250-mL] ramekins.)

In a large bowl, mix the ingredients for the topping, then spread over the apple mixture. Bake for about 45 minutes, about 25 minutes if using ramekins, until apples are tender and top is golden.

Makes 4 servings.

Chocolate Chunk Cookies

Fall brings changes in the weather and our lifestyles; when we stop gardening or biking and start hanging out in the kitchen, that means it's time to do some baking. These are yummy cookies, good companions for a cup of tea and a book on a rainy autumn afternoon.

½ cup	(125 mL) butter
1 cup	(250 mL) brown sugar
1 large	egg
2 tsp	vanilla extract
1¾ cup	(415 mL) all-purpose flour
½ tsp	baking powder
½ tsp	baking soda
½ tsp	salt
½ tsp	cinnamon
1½ tsp	instant espresso powder
2 cups	(500 mL) dark chocolate chunks
1 cup	(250 mL) pecans (optional)

Preheat oven to 300°F (150°C).

In a large bowl, cream the butter and sugar with an electric mixer until fluffy. Add the egg and vanilla and beat 30 seconds.

Sift together dry ingredients and add in 3 batches to the liquid, mixing just to blend. Add chocolate chunks. Drop the cookie dough in 2 tbsp-sized measures onto a greased cookie sheet, about 3 in (8 cm) apart. Press dough into 2-in (5-cm) circles. Bake for 20 minutes until browned at the edges.

Makes 24 cookies.

Spicy Espresso Nuts

This time of year means the arrival of fresh nuts in the shell. For this recipe, you can buy them pre-shelled at the Market. These are a great treat with a real wake-'em-up kick.

½ cup	(125 mL) white sugar
2 tbsp	finely ground espresso beans
1 tbsp	instant espresso powder
½ tsp	cinnamon
½ tsp	cayenne pepper
½ tsp	sea salt
1 large	egg white
4 cups	(1 L) mixed nuts, unsalted

Preheat oven to 325°F (160°C).

Mix the first 6 ingredients together in a small bowl. In a large bowl, beat the egg white until frothy. Add the nuts and toss to coat. Sprinkle the espresso mixture over the nuts and toss to coat. Arrange nuts in a single layer on a greased baking sheet. Bake for 5 minutes and then stir, keeping nuts in a single layer. Bake for another 5 minutes or until they are dry to the touch. Cool and store in an airtight container for up to 2 weeks.

Makes 4 cups (about 125–150 g).

PUBLIC MARKET

Winter

In the summer months or on sunny days, the Market teems with people enjoying the bustle, buskers, and general joie de vivre of West Coast living. The persona of the Market itself changes on dreary winter days. The aisles and shops can be pretty quiet. Market merchants linger over coffees and visit each other's businesses. Those in the know take advantage of the relaxed and uncrowded atmosphere, and the merchants have more time to share their extensive knowledge of their products with the customers.

But the Market gets really busy again in the last few weeks before Christmas. This is when decisions about holiday foods are made, decorating supplies are bought, and last-minute gifts picked up. The week between Christmas and New Year's is busy again when entire families come to the Market for a break from holiday dinners. The Market closes only for Christmas, Boxing Day, and New Year's Day. Come January 2, often the slowest day of the year, it's time to think about cooler cleanup and high dusting.

The tourists are wonderful, and anyone who comes to Granville Island, even for a look around or quick lunch, contributes to the great success that the Market has always enjoyed. The folks who have kept the Market flourishing over the years are too many to mention—they are the regulars. Some live in the neighbourhood, others drive in from the 'burbs to shop and relax. As merchants, we are always thrilled to see their familiar smiling faces on long wet winter days. They may order only a small coffee or purchase a few carrots, but they keep coming back. We know their likes and dislikes, have met their kids, and now their grandchildren. Some have become friends and even a few romances have bloomed; they are part of our community.

THE
PUBLIC MARKET
ON GRANVILLE ISLAND
Open/Ouvert 0900-1900 Every Day/Tous Les Jours

Appetizers & Snacks

Avocadoes

Avocadoes, which are actually a fruit, are savoured for their nutty, buttery taste that complements a variety of foods. High in fat but low in cholesterol, a 1-oz (30-g) serving (about three slices) has nearly twenty vitamins and minerals ... They're also easy to digest and kids love them.

Avocadoes should feel heavy for their size. Don't buy them if the skins have black spots; the skin should be green-black and pebbly textured. While they can mature on the tree, avocadoes soften and develop their fullest flavour after picking. When firm and green, they take three to four days to ripen. An overripe avocado has a yeasty smell, but don't throw it out—give it to your dog! Dogs have a mysterious passion for this fruit, and luckily, avocadoes' high oil content will give your dog a shiny, healthy coat.

Guacamole

The recipe for this Mexican dish can be as simple as an avocado mashed with a little salt and something acidic, like lemon or lime juice added to taste. You can also add chopped tomato, crushed or minced fresh garlic, some chopped fresh cilantro, and a choice of seasonings (cumin is often used). Serve as a dip with raw vegetables or as a spread on sandwiches. Make it thinner and more acidic and it becomes a Venezuelan sauce that's delicious served over grilled meats.

Avocado Aioli

In the past, we used mayonnaise, but blending a rich Greek-style yogurt with avocado is the new (healthier) way to make this recipe.

1	ripe avocado
	salt and freshly ground pepper, to taste
⅓ cup	(80 mL) Greek yogurt
1 tbsp	finely chopped fresh basil
2 tsp	minced garlic

Mash the avocado with the salt and pepper. Stir in the yogurt, basil, and garlic.

Makes ½ cup (125 mL).

Joe Stewart at Blackberry Books.

Soups & Salads

Orange and Pomegranate Salad

Judie created this delicious salad for the first edition of this cookbook. Combine juicy orange slices and ruby-coloured pomegranate seeds with the green lettuce to make a tonic for the senses on a cold winter's evening.

4 medium	oranges, peeled
seeds of 2	pomegranates
1 cup	(250 mL) fresh orange juice
6 tbsp	extra virgin olive oil
	salt and freshly ground pepper, to taste
4	butter lettuce hearts (the tender centre leaves)

Thinly slice peeled oranges in rounds. Place into a serving bowl and add the pomegranate seeds. In a small bowl, whisk the orange juice, olive oil, salt, and pepper. Pour over the fruit. Toss the lettuce gently with the fruit just before serving.

Makes 4 servings.

Fiona's Borscht

This inexpensive, comforting soup from Fiona McLeod, co-author of the first edition, was inspired by childhood memories of her Doukhobor neighbours. This is a vegetarian recipe made with potatoes, cabbage, and tomatoes; the beet is used as seasoning and colour. Try to use fresh or fresh-frozen dill, as it makes the flavours come to life.

3 large	potatoes, peeled and quartered
1 tbsp	butter
½ cup	(125 mL) cream
3 tbsp	butter
2 large	onions, finely chopped
1	celery stalk with leaves, finely chopped
1	green bell pepper, finely chopped
1 medium	beet, peeled and grated
1	carrot, grated
1 14-oz	(398-mL) can of tomatoes
1	bay leaf
3	potatoes, diced
1	carrot, diced
4	green onions, finely chopped
1 cup	(250 mL) finely chopped cabbage
⅓ cup	(80 mL) finely chopped dill
	salt and freshly ground pepper, to taste

Boil the 3 large potatoes in 5 cups of water until tender. Drain and reserve the water.

Mash the potatoes with 1 tbsp butter and cream and set aside.

In a large skillet on medium heat, melt 3 tbsp butter and add the onions, celery, green pepper, beet, and grated carrot. Coat with the butter and cook for 5–10 minutes. Add the can of tomatoes and bay leaf and simmer for another 15 minutes.

Place the diced potatoes and carrots with the reserved potato cooking water in a large Dutch oven on high heat and bring to a rolling boil. Add the cabbage to the soup and bring to a boil. Reduce heat to medium and add the mashed potatoes and sautéed vegetables from the skillet. Add the green onions, dill, salt, and pepper and heat for 2–5 minutes.

Makes 6–8 servings.

Seafood Chowder

This chowder takes advantage of the Market's fabulous variety of seafood vendors and the quality of their products. It makes a lovely evening meal. Many West Coast families prepare it as their traditional Christmas Eve fare.

2 tbsp	canola oil
1 medium	onion, coarsely chopped
3	celery stalks, coarsely chopped
3 medium	carrots, coarsely chopped
3 cups	(750 mL) fish stock
1 cup	(250 mL) coarsely chopped potatoes (any kind you have on hand)
1½ lb	(750 g) solid-fleshed fish filets (salmon, halibut, or cod work well)
1 14-oz	(398-mL) can baby clams
1 tbsp	finely chopped fresh dill, or 1 tsp dried
½ tsp	dried thyme
	salt and freshly ground pepper, to taste
1 cup	(250 mL) whipping cream

In a large, heavy-bottomed pot on medium-high, heat the oil. Add the onions, celery, and carrots and sauté for approximately 4 minutes, until the onions are translucent. Add the fish stock and potatoes and bring to a boil. Reduce the heat to medium-low and add the fish, clams, and seasonings. Stir in the cream and heat to serving temperature. Season to taste and serve immediately.

Makes 6 servings.

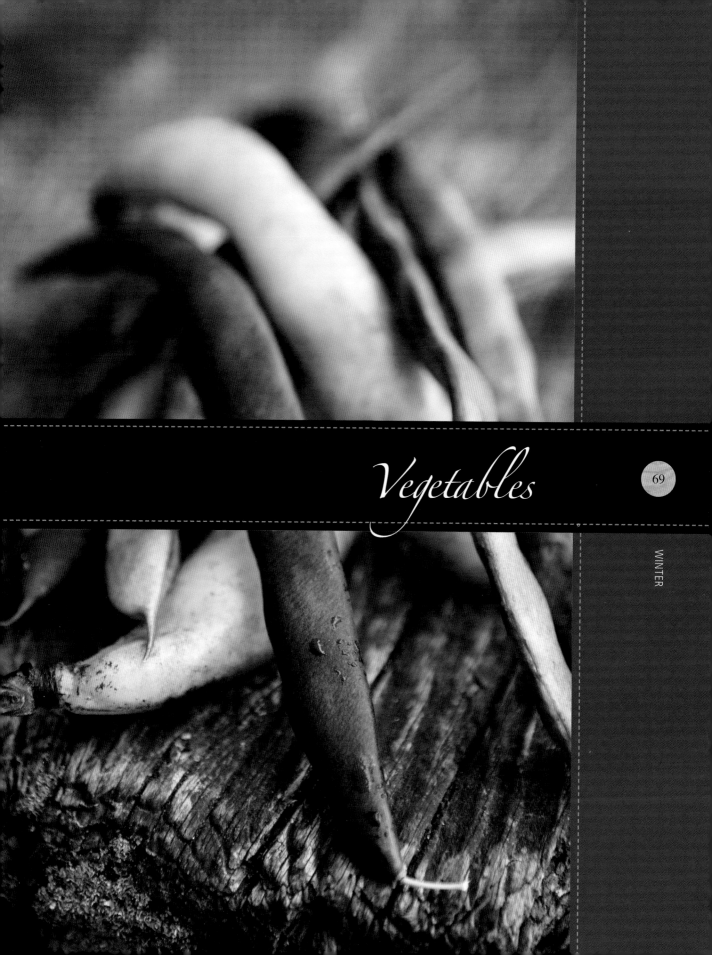

Vegetables

Duso's Classic Tomato Sauce

This is Mauro Duso's recipe for a light, refreshing alternative to the thicker, long-simmered tomato sauce. Canned tomatoes are one of the best processed foods available, and in winter they taste better and are cheaper than imported field tomatoes. Meaty Italian plum tomatoes are the best canned variety for cooking and are useful for quick sauces, curries, and soups.

3 tbsp	extra virgin olive oil
2 tbsp	butter
1 large	onion, finely chopped
2	garlic cloves, finely chopped
2 28-oz	(796 mL) cans Italian plum tomatoes
2 tbsp	tomato paste
3	bay leaves
1 tbsp	(15 mL) oregano (dried)
1 tbsp	dried basil or ½ cup fresh, finely chopped
	freshly ground pepper, to taste
1 tbsp	butter

In a large pot on medium, heat the olive oil and butter. Add the onions and garlic and sauté until translucent.

Crush the tomatoes (use your hands—it feels good!) and add to the onions along with the tomato paste, herbs, and spices. Simmer for 30 minutes, stirring occasionally. Remove from heat and stir in the butter.

Store in the refrigerator for 1 week or in the freezer for up to 6 months.

Makes 1½ qts (1½ L).

Sauté of Brussels Sprouts and Hazelnuts

This recipe originally called for broccoli, but we've changed it up for this edition. It makes an excellent side dish for poultry entrées. Here in British Columbia, hazelnuts are grown in the Fraser Valley region (although they grow wild throughout the province) and are sold at the Market.

1 lb	(500 g) Brussels sprouts (select small sprouts or cut large ones in half)
2 tbsp	butter
2 tbsp	extra virgin olive oil
¼ cup	(60 mL) toasted hazelnuts
	salt and freshly ground pepper, to taste
	juice of ½ a lemon

Steam the Brussels sprouts until tender, about 5–6 minutes. In a medium sauté pan, melt the butter then add olive oil. Add the Brussels sprouts and sauté until they begin to brown. Add the hazelnuts and stir to combine.

Remove from heat and season with salt and pepper. Squeeze lemon juice over top and serve.

Makes 4–6 servings.

WINTER

Fennel with Béchamel Sauce

We couldn't resist including this Italian classic that was provided for the first edition by the always elegant and sophisticated mother of Mauro Duso, the late Mirella Duso. Mirella was more than just Mauro's mom, she was our go-to elder. It consistently brings rave reviews.

2	fresh fennel heads

BÉCHAMEL SAUCE:

½ tbsp	butter
½ tbsp	all-purpose flour
1	cup (250 mL) whole milk
1	egg yolk, beaten

TOPPING:

1 tsp	salt
	pinch of white pepper
	pinch of ground nutmeg
3 tbsp	finely grated Parmesan cheese

Preheat oven to 400°F (200°C).

Wash and trim green stems from the fennel heads. Discard stems and cut fennel heads into quarters. Place in a heavy-bottomed sauce pan and cover with cold water. Bring to a boil, then reduce heat to medium and simmer for 15 minutes.

While fennel is boiling, prepare the Béchamel sauce: Melt the butter in a medium saucepan on medium heat. Add the flour and stir with a wooden spoon until well blended. Gradually add the milk, stirring constantly for 2 minutes. Remove from heat and whisk in egg yolk.

Drain the fennel and transfer to a buttered baking dish large enough to fit the fennel in one layer. Cover with the sauce, then sprinkle with the salt, pepper, nutmeg, and cheese. Bake for 15–20 minutes until golden.

Makes 4 servings.

Entrées

Risotto with Wild Mushrooms

Preparing a risotto is a gentle, relaxing way to transition from a busy workday into dinnertime. Use Italian Arborio rice in this recipe; it is the only kind that will create the proper texture for risotto. Known as cèpes *in France, dried Boletus (or porcini) mushrooms are a type of wild mushroom that will give your risotto a subtle and sophisticated flavour.*

½ oz	(15g) dried porcini mushrooms
¾ cup	(185 mL) white wine
2 tbsp	butter
2 cups	(500 mL) sliced fresh mushrooms (any kind)
5 cups	(1¼ L) chicken stock
2 tbsp	extra virgin olive oil
¼ cup	(60 mL) butter
1 medium	white onion, finely chopped
1 cup	(250 mL) Arborio rice

Soak the dried porcini mushrooms in wine and set aside.

In a small pan on medium, melt the 2 tbsp butter. Add the fresh mushrooms and sauté until just soft and set aside.

In a large saucepan, heat the stock to a simmer.

In a large Dutch oven on medium, heat the oil and butter until the butter is melted. Add the onions and sauté until translucent (about 2–3 minutes). Add the rice to the onions and stir gently on low heat until coated with the oil and butter and slightly translucent.

Add a ladle (about ½ cup/125 mL) of hot stock and stir constantly until the rice has absorbed most of the liquid. Repeat this process until the rice is tender on the outside and slightly firm in the middle. Remember to keep the stock hot and the risotto at a lively simmer.

Before serving, add the porcini mushrooms in wine and the sautéed mushrooms to the rice. Heat and serve.

Makes 6 servings.

Macaroni and Cheese

There are so many versions of this winter comfort-food, we wanted to provide you with a basic "home-style" recipe. Feel free to veg it up with peppers, tomatoes, or fresh herbs.

1½ cup	(375 mL) elbow macaroni or pasta tubes under 2 in (5 cm) in length, such as penne, fussili etc.
3 tbsp	butter
¼ cup	(60 mL) all-purpose flour
3 cups	(750 mL) 2% milk
1 tbsp	Dijon or other hot mustard
	a few drops of your favourite hot sauce (optional)
4 cups	(1 L) grated sharp cheddar cheese

Preheat oven to 350°F (180°C).

Butter a 3-quart (3-L) casserole dish.

In a large pot of water, boil the pasta until al dente. You may want to leave it on the firm side, as the macaroni continues to cook in the oven. Drain well.

In a medium saucepan on medium heat, melt the butter. Add the flour and stir constantly with a wire whisk for about 1 minute. Slowly add the milk, mustard, and hot sauce, whisking until it boils (about 5 minutes).

Add 2 cups of the cheese and stir with a wooden spoon until melted. Add the cooked macaroni and combine well with the cheese sauce.

Place ⅓ of the mixture into the casserole and sprinkle ⅓ of the remaining cheese over top. Repeat the process twice.

Bake for about 30 minutes or until the mixture is bubbling and the top layer of cheese is melted. Let stand to cool for 5–10 minutes before serving.

Makes 6 servings.

Latkes (Potato Pancakes)

Latkes are traditionally served during Hanukkah, the eight-day Jewish festival of lights, celebrated in November or December. People seem to eat more latkes at the beginning of the holiday, and this make-ahead recipe lets you decide how many you want to serve. (These are delicious any time; you don't have to wait for a holiday!) Serve with sour cream and apple sauce.

Here's a great tip about shredded potatoes: It's the starch in the potatoes that makes them turn grey when exposed to air. Add a tablespoon of white vinegar to each batch to prevent greying.

4 medium	potatoes (don't peel them, just give them a good scrub)
1–2 tbsp	white vinegar
1 medium	onion, diced
2 eggs	beaten
⅓ cup	(80 mL) all-purpose flour
1 tsp	baking powder (optional)
	salt and freshly ground pepper, to taste
¼ cup	(60 ml) canola oil

Cut the potatoes into large chunks. Using a food processor with a steel blade, process the potatoes until coarsely chopped. If making two batches, add 1 tbsp vinegar to each batch of potatoes. Place potatoes in a medium-sized bowl and set aside. (If you are grating the potatoes by hand, grate 2 at a time, add 1 tbsp vinegar, then grate 2 more potatoes and add another tbsp vinegar.)

Blend the onions and eggs in the food processor until well mixed, then add to the potatoes. Add the flour and baking powder and season with salt and pepper.

In a medium frying pan on medium, heat 2 tsp of the oil. Add about ¼ cup of the batter. Use a slotted spoon so that excess liquid doesn't make the latkes too wet. Cook on each side for 7–10 minutes, until brown, then set aside and drain on paper towels. Repeat with the rest of the oil and batter. Like all pancakes, the first few can be a challenge; your frying skills will improve with practice.

If you've made more latkes than can be eaten at once, place the leftovers on a tray; they can be stored in the freezer in plastic zip-lock bags for several weeks.

Makes about 24 latkes.

Judie's Meatloaf

After twenty-five-plus years, this is still Judie's go-to recipe for meatloaf. In the first edition, we were so impressed with all the new patés that were available, we called this recipe "Paté at Home (an updated Meatloaf)." This can be served with mashed potatoes and gravy made from the reserved pan juices, or be refrigerated and used later for sandwiches. Or cut the recipe in half for smaller loaves or fewer cheeseburger muffins.

4 lb	(1.8 kg) lean ground beef
¼ cup	(60 mL) Worcestershire sauce
1 medium	onion, finely chopped
½ lb	(250 g) fresh mushrooms, coarsely chopped
	salt and freshly ground pepper, to taste

Preheat oven to 350°F (180°C).

Mix all the ingredients together with your hands (this is easiest when the meat is at room temperature). Shape into a loaf and place in a roasting pan. (Alternately, make individual servings in muffin tins. Place a slice of cheese over each cup to make "cheeseburger" meatloaves.)

Bake large loaf for 1 hour, or muffin-sized loaves for 25 minutes, basting with the pan juices every 10 minutes. Drain and reserve the pan juices for gravy, if desired.

Makes 8 servings.

Sunday Chicken Dinner

The late James Barber—Vancouver food writer, chef, TV host, and devoted "foodie" in the truest sense—was a great fan and promoter of the Granville Island Market. Carol had the wonderful opportunity to act as creative coordinator for his nationally broadcast cooking show, The Urban Peasant. *James loved good simple food, and his goal was to demystify cooking.*

This roast chicken dinner is our version of a classic Jamesian recipe that reminds us to take our time and exemplifies his favourite quote: "Do the best you can with what you've got."

1	roasting chicken, approx. 4–5 lb (1.8–2.2 kg)
1 large	onion, cut into quarters
1 large	orange, cut into quarters
4	whole garlic cloves
3	carrots, cut into 2-in (5-cm) pieces
4	fresh thyme sprigs
1 tsp	salt
1 tbsp	coarsely ground pepper
½ cup	(125 mL) white wine or apple juice

Preheat oven to 350°F (180°C).

Remove gizzards or innards from the cavity and rinse the chicken thoroughly inside and out.

Stuff the cavity with the onions, orange, garlic, carrots, and thyme. Rub salt and pepper into the chicken skin.

Place the chicken in a roasting pan and pour the wine or juice over it. Roast for approximately 1–1½ hours or until the juices run clear when the skin is pierced. Let stand 10 minutes before carving.

Makes 6–8 servings.

Baked Turkey Thighs with Winter Vegetables

We like bone-in turkey thighs: as the old saying goes, "The closer to the bone, the sweeter the meat." But don't forget that bone-in poultry takes longer to cook.

4	bone-in turkey thighs, approx. ½ lb (250 g) each
1 tbsp	salt
	freshly ground pepper, to taste
2 medium	onions, cut in half
4 2-in	(5-cm) slices of winter squash
4 2-in	(5-cm) slices of parsnip or turnip
2 tbsp	extra virgin olive oil
4 tbsp	fresh herbs, such as sage and thyme, or 2 tbsp dried herbs or poultry seasoning
¼ cup	(60 mL) white wine or sake

Preheat oven to 350°F (180°C).

Season the turkey thighs with salt and pepper and place in a large roasting pan. Place the onions, squash, and parsnips or turnips in a bowl and toss in 1 tbsp olive oil. Place half an onion and 2 slices of each of the other vegetables under each thigh. Add the rest of the olive oil and the herbs over the turkey. Cover and bake for 1½ hours.

Remove cover, add wine or sake, and bake for another 15 minutes.

Turn the oven off, cover the dish, and let sit in the oven for 10 minutes before serving.

Makes 4 servings.

Turkey Then and Now

In the 1980s, when the first edition of this book came out, turkeys were mostly sold as whole birds and eaten only at Thanksgiving and Christmas. But even then, the Turkey Shop in the Market was far ahead of its time, as it sold turkey parts, ground turkey, and turkey sausages. Today, turkey is part of our everyday food choices; we think turkey chili tops the field!

The original Granville Island Market turkey man is gone; now, Jackson's Poultry offers fresh turkey to Market shoppers.

Ginger Pork in Squash

When we created this recipe in the '80s, pork was still regarded as an unhealthy protein; it was not until it was promoted as "the other white meat" that its popularity soared. With so many varieties of squash now available, you can use your imagination and create your own version of this dish.

3 lb	(1½ kg) boneless pork butt
3 medium	onions, peeled and quartered
1 tbsp	grated fresh ginger
1¼ cup	(310 mL) dry sherry or fruit juice
¼ cup	(60 mL) soy sauce
2–3	acorn squash, cut in half (each with about ½ cup/125 mL capacity) or use 4–6 halves of a larger variety of squash
1 tbsp	cornstarch
1 tbsp	cold water
1	tart green apple, cored and finely chopped
1 tbsp	lemon juice

Preheat oven to 350°F (180°C).

Trim excess fat from the pork and discard. Cut the meat into 1½-in (4-cm) cubes, and place in a single layer in a rimmed baking dish. Bake for 1½ hours, stirring occasionally. Remove from oven and drain excess fat from meat.

Mix the onions, ginger, sherry, and soy sauce with the pork. Return to the oven and bake until very tender, about 1 hour.

While the pork is baking, scoop the seeds out of the squash. Steam the squash halves in a baking pan with 1 in (2.5 cm) of water for about 30 minutes until tender.

Mix the cornstarch and water to form a paste. Remove pork mixture from oven. Add the cornstarch paste to the pork, stirring well to combine. Mound 1 cup (250 mL) pork mixture into each of the squash cavities.

Combine the chopped apple and lemon juice and spoon mixture over each squash half.

Makes 4–6 servings.

Cobb Panini

There are dozens of ways to enjoy leftovers from your roast chicken dinner. We love this sandwich (inspired by the traditional Cobb salad), and it's always a big hit. If you have the ingredients on hand, it's not as ambitious as it sounds.

2 tbsp	mayonnaise
	French baguette or 2 ciabatta buns, cut in half, or 4 slices bread
2 oz	(60 g) blue cheese
½	ripe avocado
4 slices	cooked bacon
4 oz	(115g) cooked chicken, sliced or shredded

Preheat oven to 350°F (180°C).

Spread the mayo on both halves of the baguette or buns, or on bread. Crumble blue cheese onto one of the baguette or bun halves or 2 slices of the bread. Slice avocado thin and place slices on top of the blue cheese. Place the bacon slices and chicken on top of the avocado and then close the sandwich with the other half of the baguette, buns, or bread. Toast in a panini machine or wrap in foil and bake for 10 minutes.

Makes 2 sandwiches.

Alvin George is the baker at Lee's Donuts.

Fruits, Sweets, & Baked Goods

Healthy Irish Soda Bread

We love soda bread with soup or stew; a warm, just-out-of-the-oven loaf can't be beat. Once we stocked all the ingredients for this recipe into our pantry, we found that we were inspired to make it on a regular basis.

1¾ cups	(415 mL) whole wheat flour	1 tsp	baking soda
1¾ cups	(415 mL) enriched white flour	1 tsp	sea salt
3 tbsp	toasted wheat bran	2 tbsp	cold butter (cut into pieces)
2 tbsp	wheat germ	2 cups	(500 mL) whole milk
2 tbsp	rolled oats	1 tbsp	white vinegar
2 tbsp	brown sugar		

Preheat oven to 425°F (220°C).

Grease a 9 x 5 x 3-in (2-L) loaf pan.

Combine the dry ingredients and mix well. Cut into the butter until mixture resembles a course meal. Add the milk and vinegar, and stir to form a soft dough.

Place in loaf pan and bake for about 45 minutes, until a toothpick inserted in the centre comes out clean. Remove from pan and cool on a wire rack.

Makes 1 loaf.

When Bread Got Better

"White or brown?" Our choices are not so simple anymore. Now we're more likely to be asked if we want fig and anise with walnut, white chocolate with blueberries, or apple focaccia.

The first Market bakery was Stuart's. There were also the specialty shops: Tino's Italian Bakery, Bageland, the Muffin Granny, and Lee's Donuts. These were the predecessors of the ultra-chic artisan Terra Breads and La Baguette & L'Echalote. Stuart's is still at the Market and still keeping pace with the trends.

Forget the cake, let's eat bread!

McLeod Marmalade

An heirloom recipe from the first edition's co-author Fiona McLeod. The tangy taste of this marmalade comes from tart Seville oranges, which have a very short season in January. If you don't see them, be sure to ask the Market produce vendors when they'll be available. Summer jam-makers, take note—here's your winter-only jamming opportunity.

3 lb	(1½ kg) Seville oranges
1	lemon
3 oz	(90 g) fresh ginger root, finely chopped
8 cups	(2 L) sugar or 4 cups (1 L) honey
1 tbsp	molasses
6 tbsp	orange liqueur or brandy (optional)

Preheat oven to 200°F (95°C).

Scrub the oranges and lemon with a stiff brush under running water to clean them. Place in a large bowl and cover the with boiling water. Let stand for 2–3 minutes. Peel the oranges and lemon and roughly chop the peel. Remove the pith and seeds from the fruit and cut into segments.

Place the seeds, pith, and ginger into a cheesecloth bag and secure the top. Place fruit, peels, and cheesecloth bag in a large pot and add about 3 qt (3 L) water. Bring to a boil and simmer for 2–3 hours.

When liquid in the pot is reduced to ⅔ of its original level, remove from heat. Remove the bag and squeeze out excess liquid into the pot.

Add the honey or sugar and the molasses to the mixture. Bring back to a boil and add liqueur, if using. After 15 minutes, put a small amount of the marmalade on a spoon, let cool, and turn the spoon over. When the mixture falls from the spoon in a single drop, the marmalade has jelled. Until this stage is reached, continue to boil; check mixture every 5 minutes.

Remove from heat and skim off foam with a spoon that has been run under hot water.

Let mixture stand about 10 minutes until a skin has formed, and stir gently to mix the peel evenly.

Pour the marmalade into sterilized jars and seal in a canner as per the manufacturer's instructions.

Makes 20 8-oz (250-mL) jars.

Sticky Toffee Muffin Cups

A wonderful winter Saturday night dessert to accompany an at-home movie, this is an easy version of traditional sticky toffee pudding. The rich caramel sauce (recipe follows) also goes well with whipped or ice cream.

1¼ cups	(310 mL) finely chopped dates
2 tbsp	instant coffee granules
1 cup	(250 mL) boiling water
½ cup	(125 mL) butter, room temperature
1 cup	(250 mL) brown sugar
4 large	eggs
1¾ cups	(415 mL) self-rising flour
1 tsp	baking soda
2 tbsp	orange zest (optional)

Place the dates in a small bowl. Stir coffee granules into the boiling water. Pour over the dates and let cool for 1 hour.

Preheat oven to 350°F (180°C).

Grease and flour a 12-cup muffin tin.

In a large bowl, beat the butter and sugar until well-blended. Add 2 eggs, one at a time, beating well after each addition. Add half the flour and blend. Add the other 2 eggs, again one at a time, and beat well after each addition. Add remaining flour and blend. Stir the baking soda and orange zest (if using) into the date/coffee mixture, then add to the batter and blend.

Pour batter into the muffin cups and bake for approximately 1 hour, or until a toothpick inserted into the centre comes out clean. Cool on a wire rack until just warm and un-mold onto plates. Serve topped with Caramel Sauce (p. 90).

Makes 12 muffin cups.

Caramel Sauce

Easty to prepare, this rich sauce completes the Sticky Toffee Muffin Cups (p. 88).

1 cup	(250 mL) brown sugar
¼ cup	(60 mL) butter
½ cup	(125 mL) whipping cream

In a heavy-bottomed saucepan on medium heat, melt the butter and sugar together. Slowly add the cream and stir until mixed. Let cool slightly and pour over muffin cups. (Also delicious over ice cream!)

Makes about ¾ cup.

One thing you should know about buskers

A regular busker in the courtyard outside the Market had a routine in which he would take people's watches without them noticing. Of course, he always returned them at the end of his act—except to the guy who left early. Moral of the story: stay until the end of the act!

Coffee evolution

When Carol started the Blue Parrot Espresso Bar at Granville Island Market, the Italian coffee shops on Commercial Drive were the only other places in Vancouver sporting espresso machines. The Blue Parrot was the first coffee bar with a great view—both outside and inside.

In the 1970s, fancy dessert coffees with whipped cream and liqueur were the big thing, and many customers didn't know what espresso was all about, so the staff had to give a few crash courses every day. But our customers would often stare unhappily at the tiny cup in a manner the staff soon designated "the look." After a quick explanation, many chose lattes or cappuccinos for their introductory beverage. Although the Blue Parrot served only a few drink options—espresso, cappuccino, latte, and chocolate mocha—the response was huge, and soon Vancouverites joined the coffee-culture phenomenon that began in Seattle at Starbucks.

While we are now accustomed to seeing people rushing around town with enormous paper cups brimming with frapped, blended, and variously altered versions of espresso, in the Market's early years, the Blue Parrot didn't offer take-away; coffee lovers didn't complain, as they enjoyed the social aspects of the experience. And today, the "gang" of familiar faces still keeps filling up the stools at the Blue Parrot's counter. Carol and her staff made so many good friends there—mostly other merchants, but also regular customers, who were welcomed each and every morning.

Rugelach

Winter holidays wouldn't be the same without traditional nut-and-dried-fruit recipes. A Hanukkah staple, rugelach cookies feature these tasty treats.

1 cup	(250 mL) unsalted butter, cold
8 oz	(230 g) cream cheese
2 cups	(500 mL) all-purpose flour
¼ tsp	salt
⅓ cup	(80 mL) sour cream
½ cup	(125 mL) white sugar
1 cup	(250 mL) walnuts, finely chopped
1 tbsp	ground cinnamon
½ cup	(125 mL) raisins

Preheat oven to 350°F (180°C).

Cut the butter and cream cheese into 1-in (2.5 cm) cubes. In a food processor, pulse the butter and cream cheese together with the flour, salt, and sour cream until it forms a crumbly mixture.

Divide the dough into 4 parts and, with your hands, flatten into disks. Wrap each one in plastic wrap and chill in refrigerator for at least 2 hours.

Work with one disk of dough at a time and keep the rest refrigerated. Roll into a 9-in (23-cm) round shape. Combine the sugar, cinnamon, walnuts, and raisins. Sprinkle with ¼ of the sugar mixture and press these lightly into the dough. Cut into 12 wedges. Roll up the wedges, starting from the wide end, and form into a crescent shape. Repeat this process with all the disks of dough.

Place on an ungreased cookie sheet and chill in refrigerator for 20 minutes. Bake for 20–25 minutes, or until golden.

Makes about 48 cookies.

Mexican Wedding Cakes

These "cakes" are really festive shortbread cookies which seem to be everyone's favourite during the holiday season. The icing sugar coating is optional.

1 cup	(250 mL) butter, room temperature
½ cup	(125 mL) powdered or icing sugar
2 tsp	vanilla extract
1 cup	(250 mL) finely chopped walnuts or almonds
2 cups	(500 mL) all-purpose flour
½ cup	(125 mL) icing sugar, to coat (optional)

Preheat oven to 325°F (160°C)

In a medium-sized bowl, cream the butter and sugar. Add the vanilla extract and blend well. Add the nuts and flour and stir until blended. Cover and chill for 3–4 hours.

Shape the dough into walnut-sized balls. Place on an ungreased cookie sheet and bake for 15–20 minutes until slightly browned. Cool on a wire rack. When cool, roll the cookies in icing sugar if desired.

Makes about 18 cookies.

All in the family

The Granville Island Public Market was known from the start as a place where small, locally owned food businesses flourished. There were no franchises in the Market, and owner-operators were the norm. As we got to know our customers and their families, they, in turn, became familiar with us and our families. Many customers came from the Gastown Market where Judie and Fred Glick had a produce stall in the late '70s, and they became the "regulars."

Most of these customers just assumed staff members were part of the family. This led to jokes and sometimes silly assumptions. Jerry Tran, who has worked at Duso's Italian Foods for many years, has family connections in the Market: his father baked for La Baguette until he retired. Jerry is great with customers and a real storyteller. One day, a childhood friend of Mauro Duso's visited the Market when Mauro wasn't there. At the end of a lively conversation, Jerry told this man that he was Mauro's adopted son from Vietnam. When the visitor finally got in touch with Mauro a few months later, he mentioned meeting the adopted son—who Mauro knew nothing about! While Jerry's tale was a little tall, some staff did indeed become family through work at Duso's. Both Susan Foot and her brother Mike met their mates while working there; Susan, in fact, married the boss.

After thirty years, the Market is seeing the next generation of vendors as kids take over businesses from their parents. Does the kid behind the counter look familiar? Maybe his or her mom or dad served you ten or twenty years ago.

Fred and Judie Glick at their produce stand in 1979.

January Fruit Salad

Eating seasonally and locally is—as Martha Stewart says—"a very good thing" for farmers, the economy, the environment, and even for tourism. Because Granville Island is a fresh food market, in January we enjoy other people's local produce, like Indian River grapefruit from Florida, Hawaiian avocadoes, and apple bananas. A taste of these will make you feel as warm and sunny as the places they come from! Serve this fruit salad with vanilla yogurt.

1	pink grapefruit, peeled and cut into sections
2	apple bananas, sliced
4	kumquats, seeded and cut into slivers
1 cup	(250 mL) pineapple chunks

Combine all the ingredients in a bowl and let the flavours marry before serving.

Makes 4 servings.

Was that you pounding on the front door to the Market that first Monday in January?

The market closes on Mondays for the entire month of January for major cleaning and repairs. Janitors work in shifts around the clock every day of the week, but January Mondays are different. The big coolers where merchants stock produce need to be cleaned out, washed, repaired, and put back to work. Individual merchants can use this time to make repairs as well: new display cases arrive, signs are painted, and equipment is updated. The art of "high dusting" the top of the Market interior requires special equipment to be brought in. By the end of January, when the cleaning is complete, the winter sky starts to show more light, and the Market heads toward spring.

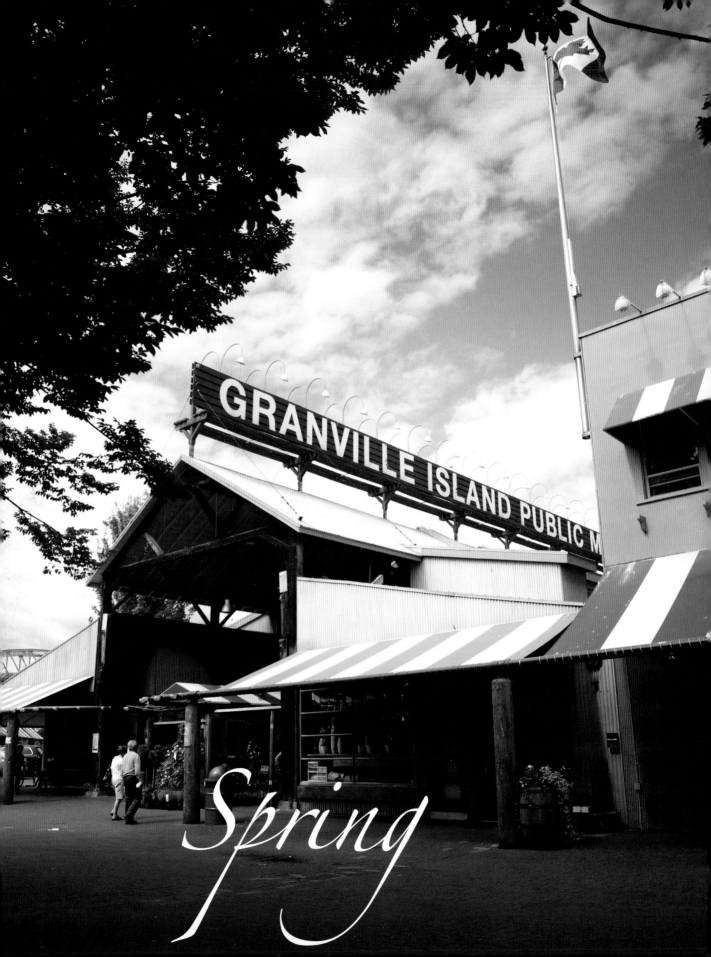

Spring

The Japanese word "shun" describes what is plentiful, inexpensive, and fresh. Usually applied to food, this term is used in ikebana (the Japanese art of flower arranging) as well. There is delight in food when it is within the cycle of nature, just as there is in the annual glory of cherry blossoms and tulips in Vancouver each spring.

Spring starts the abundance of fresh and local produce as the Market captures the feel of the changing seasons. Spot prawns, sockeye salmon, and local berries all begin to appear as we enjoy fresh salads and the first barbecues of the year. The day tables are filled with daffodils that brighten the aisles; plant vendors bring in their supplies of seedlings, flowers, and vegetables for our planters, window boxes, and gardens.

The Market courtyard is packed with people drawn outside by the warmer weather; extra outdoor furniture appears to accommodate the crowds. Market staff add new flora to the planters and hanging baskets, and the seagulls and pigeons arrive to greet the latest crop of kids who love to feed and chase the birds for hours.

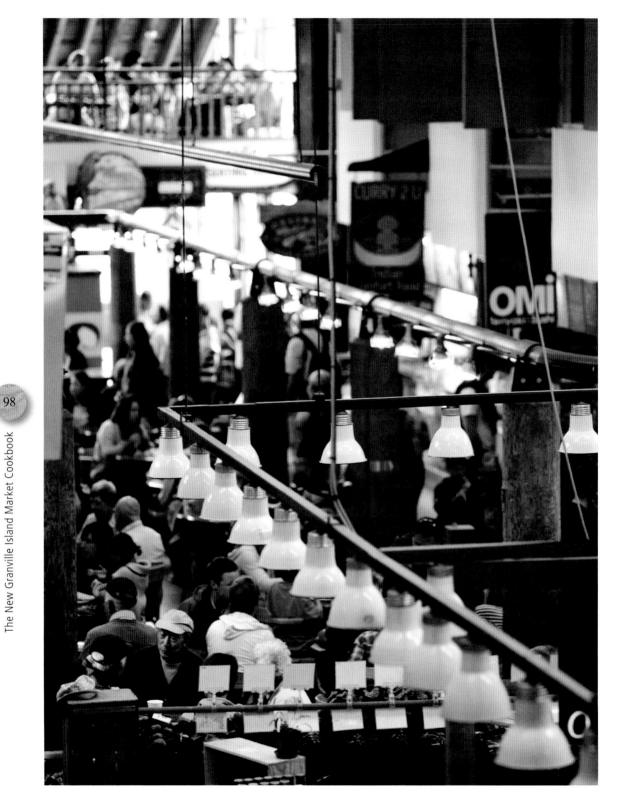

The New Granville Island Market Cookbook

Appetizers & Snacks

Mango Salsa

If a mango smells really good, it's ripe and ready to eat. This salsa goes with fish, with pork—with just about everything.

2 large	ripe mangoes, peeled and coarsely chopped
½ medium	red onion, finely chopped
½	red bell pepper, finely chopped
1	serrano or jalapeño pepper, seeded and minced
	juice and zest of 1 lime

Combine all the ingredients in a non-reactive (glass) bowl, mix well, and serve immediately.

Makes 1½ cups (375 mL).

Salsas

Salsa can really ramp up an everyday meal into something special. So many delicious combinations of fruits and vegetables fall under the salsa "umbrella." We've provided a couple of recipes derived from the basic Mexican template; these are in the salsa *cruda* (raw) and *picada* (chopped) categories. Feel free to use your imagination and talents to create your own favourite variations.

Remember to be very careful when handling the hot peppers. Latex gloves will protect your hands; try not to touch your skin, especially near your eyes, until after you've taken off the gloves and washed your hands!

Tomato Salsa

Although tomato salsa is usually served with tortilla chips, we think spears of Belgian endive or celery sticks provide a healthier alternative for dipping. This is also a great condiment for grilled chicken or pork.

3 large	firm ripe tomatoes, coarsely chopped
1 medium	red onion, finely chopped
¼ cup	(60 mL) fresh cilantro, finely chopped
2	jalapeño peppers, seeded and minced, or a few dashes of your favourite hot sauce
1 tbsp	extra virgin olive oil

Combine all the ingredients in a glass bowl, mix well, and serve immediately.

Makes about 2 cups (500 mL).

Calamari

When we looked back on this recipe from the original book, we almost decided to exclude it—does anyone cook squid at home? But if you enjoy these tender crisp morsels in restaurants, you should know how easily and inexpensively calamari can be prepared at home. Granville Island Market's original smoke shop vendor Voula Garifaldis, still our mentor for Greek food, says the two secrets of tender calamari are 1) marinating the cleaned squid for as long as possible (at least 2 hours) and 2) making sure that the cooking oil is hot. (Note: A cooking thermometer is useful for testing the temperature of the oil.) Serve garnished with lemon, onions, and parsley.

We've included a recipe for tzatziki, a "must have" dipping sauce for the squid.

12	squid (cleaned) and cut crosswise to make ¾-in (2-cm) wide rings (cut the tentacles into 2 or 3 pieces if they are large)
½ cup	(125 mL) lemon juice
½ cup	(125 mL) extra virgin olive oil
2 cups	(500 mL) vegetable oil, for frying
1	(250 mL) cup white flour
1 tsp	salt
1 tsp	freshly ground pepper
¼ cup	(60 mL) finely chopped white onion
2 tbsp	finely chopped parsley
1	lemon, cut into 4 wedges

Place the squid in a glass bowl and cover with the lemon juice and olive oil. Marinate for at least 2 hours. Remove from marinade and pat dry with a paper towel.

Pour the vegetable oil into a deep skillet or wok to a depth of 1 in (2.5 cm). Heat until oil reaches 350°F (180°C); it will give off a faint haze. You can also test the oil by dropping in a bread cube; it should be golden in about 1 minute.

Dredge the squid in the flour and season with salt and pepper. Drop the squid into the oil, one layer at a time. Turn occasionally until crisp and golden, about 3 minutes. Garnish with onions and parsley and serve with lemon wedges

Makes 4 servings.

Tzatziki

The must-have condiment for deep-fried calamari.

2 cups	(500 mL) plain whole milk yogurt (we prefer Greek yogurt)
1	English cucumber, grated
½ tsp	salt
2	garlic cloves, grated or finely minced
1 tbsp	vegetable oil
1 tsp	salt

Drain the yogurt in a colander lined with cheesecloth or paper coffee filters. Let drain for at least 3 hours, preferably overnight.

Grate the cucumber and place in a large sieve. Sprinkle with the ½ tsp salt and let drain for half an hour. Squeeze out excess moisture, then add the cucumber, garlic, oil, and 1 tsp salt to the yogurt. Mix well to combine.

Makes 2 ½ cups (625 mL).

Chicken Satay

This perennially popular Southeast Asian recipe is super easy. You can make it as spicy as you want by adjusting the amount of chilies or hot sauce in the marinade or the peanut dipping sauce. (Note: You will need bamboo skewers.)

MARINADE:

1 tbsp	canola oil
1 tbsp	sesame oil
1 tsp	hot chili paste or hot sauce
1 tbsp	soy sauce
2 tsp	minced fresh ginger root
1 tbsp	minced fresh garlic
4	boneless skinless chicken breasts or 8 boneless skinless thighs, cut into 1-in (2.5-cm) pieces

Preheat oven to 375°F (190°C).

Combine all the marinade ingredients in a medium bowl. Toss chicken pieces in marinade until well-coated and refrigerate for 1–2 hours. At the same time, soak 8–12 bamboo skewers in water for 1–2 hours.

Thread the marinated chicken onto the skewers and place on a foil-lined baking sheet. Bake for 10–15 minutes. Remove from the oven and serve immediately with the peanut dipping sauce (recipe opposite).

Makes 4 servings.

Peanut Dipping Sauce

If you use a commercial peanut butter that isn't "natural" or organic, it will contain enough sugar that you don't need to add any to this recipe. If the sauce seems too thick, thin it out with a bit of hot water. If you have only natural peanut butter, add a tsp of sugar or honey to the mixture.

4 tbsp	smooth peanut butter		1 tbsp	hoisin sauce
1 tbsp	sesame oil			zest and juice of 1 lime
1 tsp	hot chili paste			

Mix all ingredients together until well blended. This will keep for 1–2 days in the refrigerator.

Makes about ½ cup.

Flower power

Peter Rundje at V & J Plants.

Flower shops adorn the two main entrances to the Granville Island Public Market. Cut flowers, plants, and seasonal specialties like orange-lantern plants in the fall and an assortment of greens for the winter holidays can slow your walk as you take in the colourful displays. While shopping in the Market for food to enjoy with family and friends, be sure to pick up a bouquet that will brighten and inspire your dinner table.

Chef Claire's Crab Cakes

Claire May started her catering career in a small space on Granville Island and was a great customer and friend to the Market merchants. She has since moved her successful Chef Claire boutique storefront to Vancouver's trendy Main Street but still frequents the Market for ingredients for her innovative and glorious recipes. We are delighted that she's agreed to share her crab cake recipe. Serve with mango chutney (p. 20) or chipotle mayonnaise.

1 lb	(500 g) fresh cooked Dungeness crab meat
1 cup	(250 mL) breadcrumbs
1 cup	(250 mL) mayonnaise
1 tbsp	grainy mustard
1	egg yolk
¼ cup	(60 mL) finely chopped shallots
⅓ cup	(80 mL) finely chopped red bell peppers
¼ cup	(60 mL) finely chopped celery stalks
1 tbsp	finely chopped fresh thyme leaves
2 tbsp	canola oil, for frying

Preheat oven to 350°F (180°C).

Check the crabmeat to make sure all small pieces of shell have been removed. In a small bowl, mix the crab and breadcrumbs together. In a large bowl, whisk together the mayonnaise, mustard, and egg yolk. Fold in the crab mixture and the rest of the ingredients, except for the oil. Form into golf ball-sized balls and press to make patties.

In a large non-stick frying pan on medium, heat the oil. Fry the patties for about 8 minutes on each side, until brown. Transfer to a greased or parchment-lined baking sheet and bake for 5–8 minutes.

Makes 8 servings.

Cheese

It was not easy to find locally made cheese in Vancouver twenty-five years ago. One dairy farmer from the Fraser Valley sold a hard cheese that was flavoured with caraway seeds or pepper. Even Winnipeg cream cheese seemed pretty exotic, and we were still discovering Parmesan. In the mid-1990s, we began our devotion to the varieties of goat cheese with one made by the Salt Spring Island Cheese Company. Today, there's a large selection of local cheeses available at the Public Market. (And you can find two great recipes for homemade cheeses on following two pages.)

Cheese tips:

To bring out the best flavour, serve cheese at room temperature; remove it from the refrigerator thirty to sixty minutes prior to serving. Hard cheeses require a longer time to reach room temperature than soft-ripened ones. Keep the cheese wrapped so it doesn't dry out; unwrap it just before serving. Soft cheeses are easier to slice while they are still cold, so you may wish to slice them before bringing them to room temperature. If you are presenting various types of cheeses on one platter, however, you can let your guests slice their own portions. Wrap and refrigerate any leftover cheese as soon as possible, and always use fresh wrapping.

Homemade Mascarpone

If you love mascarpone but can't use the large container it comes in, make your own. Similar to crème fraîche, the cream is combined with tartaric or citric acid (in this recipe, in the form of lemon juice), then boiled, cooled, and strained. Serve over fruit, stirred into cocoa or coffee, or use instead of butter or Parmesan in a risotto (p. 74). Note: *You will need a cooking thermometer for this recipe.*

1 cup	(250 mL) heavy cream, 25 or 32 percent
½ cup	(125 mL) 6 percent cream or half and half
½ tsp	(2.5 mL) lemon juice

Warm the heavy cream in a double boiler or thick-bottomed pot. Add the 6 percent cream and heat to 185°F (85°C). Stir in the lemon juice. The cream will thicken slightly, almost immediately. Mix thoroughly. Keep the temperature at 185° for 5 minutes. Stir occasionally. Remove from heat and cool. Place the mixture into a cheesecloth, moistened coffee filter, or paper towel suspended over a bowl. Drain in refrigerator overnight.

Makes approx. 1 cup.

108

Homemade Cottage Cheese

You may ask why anyone would want to make their own cottage cheese. We say it's the reason anyone wants to make anything at home: you have control over the ingredients and the freshness can't be beat. It takes time to make but is easy to do. Enjoy it cold, at room temperature, or make Traditional Cottage Cheese Cake (p. 138) with it.

4¼ cups (1.1 L) buttermilk (organic, if possible)

Heat the buttermilk in a large enamel or Pyrex or other non-reactive pot on low heat for 15 minutes. Do not let it boil. If it starts to bubble, reduce heat. Watch the pot for another 5 minutes until the whey (the watery part of the milk) separates completely. Cool overnight at room temperature; do not refrigerate.

In the morning, line a colander with a cheesecloth and place in a large pan. Pour the buttermilk mixture into the cheesecloth. Tie ends of cheesecloth together and let drain at room temperature for the day (8 hours).

Stored in a sealed container and refrigerate.

Makes approx. 4 cups.

Soups & Salads

Strawberry Salad with Balsamic Dressing

Strawberries are usually the first fresh local berries of the season to arrive at the Market. This spring salad has retained its popularity since we included it in the first edition and goes well with a simple lunch of cheese and bread. Use any type of sugar except icing or confectionary sugar.

1 lb	(500 g) fresh strawberries, hulled and sliced
¼ cup	(60 mL) balsamic vinegar
¼ cup	(60 mL) sugar

Place the strawberries in a bowl and sprinkle with the balsamic vinegar. Let stand for 1–2 but not more than 4 hours. Sprinkle with sugar and serve immediately.

Makes 4 servings.

Asian Spinach Salad

This simple salad is an old favourite that's great to take to a picnic or potluck dinner.

1 tbsp	canola oil
1 tbsp	sesame oil
1 tbsp	rice wine vinegar
1 tbsp	soy sauce
4 cups	(1 L) fresh spinach, washed and drained well
1 cup	(250 mL) fresh bean sprouts
½	(125 mL) cup sliced almonds
½ medium	red onion, thinly sliced

Whisk the oils, vinegar, and soy sauce together in a small bowl.

Place the spinach in a large serving bowl and toss with the dressing. Add the rest of the ingredients to the salad and gently toss. Serve immediately.

Serves 4–6.

Spring Pea Soup

If you love pea soup, this is a nice light version that's perfect for warmer weather. Don't feel bad about using frozen peas as they are often frozen soon after picking and retain their freshness.

1 tbsp	extra virgin olive oil
1 medium	onion, finely chopped
4	stalks celery, finely chopped
2 large	carrots, finely chopped
4 cups	(1 L) vegetable or chicken stock
3 cups	(750 mL) peas, fresh or frozen
¼ cup	(60 mL) fresh mint leaves, finely chopped
2 tsp	salt
2 tsp	freshly ground pepper
¼ cup	(60 mL) sour cream for garnish

In a medium saucepan on medium, heat the olive oil. Add the onions, celery, and carrots and sauté for about 5 minutes. Add the stock and peas and bring to a boil. Add the mint, salt, and pepper and simmer for about 10 minutes over low heat. Transfer the soup to a blender or food processor (you can also use a hand blender) and purée until smooth (be careful when blending hot liquids). Serve warm and garnish each bowl with a tablespoon of sour cream.

Makes 8 servings.

Spring Vegetable Soup

As the weather gets warmer, many of us begin thinking about summer clothes and lighter food choices. This delicious soup still warms you up on cool spring days and fills you with all the right vegetables. It makes a lovely lunch or light supper, served with a green salad and some crusty bread.

1 tbsp	extra virgin olive oil
¼ cup	(60 mL) diced onion
½ cup	(125 mL) diced carrots
¼ cup	(60 mL) diced celery
2	garlic cloves, minced
1 qt	(1 L) chicken stock
2 tbsp	tomato paste
½ cup	(125 mL) roughly chopped Swiss chard
½ cup	(125 mL) fresh peas
2 tbsp	fresh finely chopped oregano or ½ tsp (2 mL) dried
	salt and freshly ground pepper, to taste
1 tbsp	pesto (p. 148)
1 tbsp	grated Parmesan cheese

In a large saucepan on medium, heat the oil. Add the onions, carrots, celery, and garlic and sauté until softened. Add the stock and tomato paste and bring to a boil. Reduce heat, add the chard, peas, and oregano, and simmer for about 15 minutes. Season with salt and pepper.

Serve with a dollop of pesto and a sprinkle of Parmesan cheese.

Makes 4 servings.

Entrées

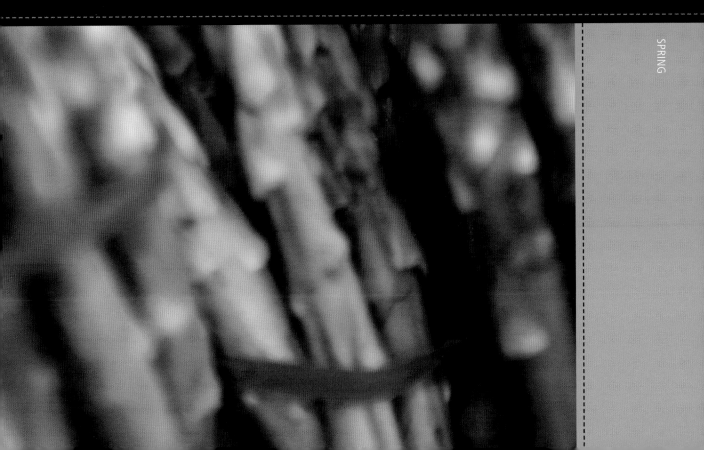

Asparagus with Fusilli

This dish tastes as good as it looks and makes a light meal or wonderful accompaniment to a heavier main dish such as steak.

½ lb   (250 g) dried fusilli

1 lb   (250 g) fresh asparagus

2 tbsp   extra virgin olive oil

2 tbsp   unsalted butter

½ cup   (125 mL) grated Parmesan cheese

In a large pot of boiling water, cook the fusilli until tender.

While the pasta is cooking, prepare the asparagus by rinsing it under cold water and snapping off the woody ends. Cut asparagus stalks into ½-in (1-cm) pieces.

In a medium frying pan on medium, heat the oil and butter until butter is just melted. Add the asparagus and sauté until tender, about 8–10 minutes.

Drain the pasta and place in a large bowl. Toss asparagus and cheese with pasta and serve immediately.

Makes 2 servings for a main course or 4 as a side dish.

Asparagus

Asparagus is harvested in the spring. Spear size has no relation to tenderness, which is determined by how the plant is grown and how soon it is eaten after harvesting.

Choose firm straight stalks with tightly closed buds. Avoid limp, wilted spears and those that are flat or angular. Don't wash asparagus before storing. It will last in the refrigerator for only about 2–3 days, so use it as soon as possible. Before cooking, bend the bottoms of each stalk until it naturally snaps off, separating tender part of the stems from the woody ends. (The ends can be used to make soup stock.)

Judie's Favourite Spot Prawns

Spot prawns are delicate, and it's important not to overcook them. Simply pop everything into a hot pan for only a few minutes.

2 lb	(1 kg) fresh whole spot prawns (head on)
2 tbsp	extra virgin olive oil
1 tbsp	finely chopped sun-dried tomatoes
1 tbsp	minced garlic
1 tsp	herbes de Provence
	salt and freshly ground pepper, to taste

To quickly peel and devein prawns before cooking, use kitchen scissors and cut down the middle of the back shell to the tail tip. Break open the shell and pull it off, leaving the tail intact. Wash or remove the black vein. You can enjoy the heads of these delicacies, so leave them on.

In a medium-sized frying pan on medium, heat the oil. Add the prawns and all other ingredients and quickly sauté for 1–2 minutes—no more, or they will get tough.

Makes 2 servings.

All About Prawns

When the Granville Island Public Market was still in its infancy in the 1980s, local prawns could only be purchased in commercial fishing communities outside British Columbia's Lower Mainland; most restaurants and individuals bought frozen imported shellfish instead. The Spot Prawn Festival, held near Granville Island, started in 2006. As Vancouver's first day-boat fishery product (local day boats leave the pier daily and return each afternoon with their catch), spot prawns are now available in the Market by two p.m. each day for about six to eight weeks during the spring and early summer. These environmentally sound, locally sourced prawns are the largest of several species of shrimp found on the Canadian west coast. Ninety percent of the catch is frozen and sent to Japan.

Whole or peeled and deveined? It's a personal choice—just enjoy these succulent creatures.

Prawns Niçoise with Penne

These sweet, succulent fresh prawns are accompanied by a tangy, hearty tomato and garlic sauce. They go perfectly with a heavier pasta such as penne—but experiment with the many different shapes and varieties available.

1 tbsp	butter
1 tbsp	extra virgin olive oil
1	small onion, finely chopped
2–3	garlic cloves, finely chopped
1	28-oz (796-mL) tin whole Italian plum tomatoes, drained and chopped (reserve liquid)
¼ tsp	dried thyme
2 tbsp	finely chopped fresh parsley
2 tsp	Pernod
¾	pound (375 g) dried penne pasta
2 tbsp	(30 mL) butter
24	large fresh prawns, peeled and deveined
6–12	Portuguese black olives, pitted and halved

In a large frying pan on medium heat, melt 1 tbsp butter with the olive oil. Add the onions and sauté until golden. Add the garlic, tomatoes, thyme, parsley, and Pernod and bring to a boil, reducing the liquid until it barely covers the solids, about 10 minutes.

Add the reserved tomato juice, lower heat, and simmer for 30 minutes. In a large pot of boiling water, cook the penne until tender, about 10 minutes.

Meanwhile, melt 2 tbsp butter in a small frying pan. Add the prawns and sauté for 3–4 minutes on high heat. Add the prawns and pan juices to the tomato sauce and allow the flavours to marry for a few minutes. Add the olives.

Drain the pasta. Serve sauce over top.

Makes 4 servings.

Jim and Scott Moorhead from Longliner Seafoods.

Spring Salmon Dinner in Eight Minutes

The delicate flavour of the fresh, champagne-coloured spring salmon stands on its own, so steam rather than poach it. Serve with a squeeze of fresh lemon and garnish with a few sprigs of fresh dill.

1 tsp	salt
3 whole	garlic cloves
10 whole	peppercorns
1 cup	(250 mL) chopped fresh dill
4	salmon steaks, 1½-in (4-cm) thick
12 whole	baby carrots or 2 cups (250 mL) carrots cut in 2-in (5-cm) diagonal slices
1 lb	(500 g) snow peas, washed and trimmed (ends and strings removed)

Place a steam basket in a large pot and add cold water to just below the bottom of the basket. Add the salt, garlic, peppercorns, and dill to the water on medium heat and bring to a boil. Place the salmon steaks in the basket. Cover pot and steam for 2 minutes. Add the carrots to the basket and steam for an additional 4 minutes. Add the snow peas and steam for an additional 2 minutes.

Makes 4 servings.

Steaming Fish

After years of grilling salmon, we found that this recipe is a refreshing way to say hello to the first salmon of the year. Fish steaks (with bones) or fillets (without bones) turn out well when cooked in an ordinary steam basket (the kind with perforated, overlapping petals). If you decide that steam cooking is definitely for you, consider a multi-layered aluminum steamer. This item, though expensive, is convenient because you can stack a whole meal in it and steam it in a matter of minutes.

To steam salmon (or any food), simply bring water to a boil in the pot, place the food in a rack over (not in) the boiling water, and cover tightly.

Miso Black Cod

Black cod is sometimes called butterfish (not to be confused with American butterfish, Peprilus triacan-thus*), which perfectly describes its mouthfeel. Also referred to as Alaskan black cod and sablefish, it has very white flesh with black skin. Harvested in the waters off the coast of British Columbia, it is considered a sustainable fishery and hence safe to eat. (*Note: *Do not use smoked black cod in this recipe.)*

MARINADE:

2 tsp	white miso
1 tbsp	mirin (rice wine)
1 tbsp	canola oil
1 tsp	apple cider vinegar

2 4-oz	(115-g) black cod fillets

Mix marinade ingredients together in a glass pie dish. Marinate the fish, skin side up, for at least half an hour.

Preheat oven to 350°F (180°C).

Bake the fish in the marinade for about 10 minutes, or until flesh is flaky.

Makes 2 servings.

Omelette with Herbs

A riff on the classic French recipe for omelette aux fines herbes *(sounds like a painting), this is a fresh and elegant way to serve eggs—perfect for a spring lunch paired with a green salad and some delicious bread fresh from the bakery. A famous chef once said everyone should know how to make an omelette for the person they slept with the night before. Here's your chance.*

1 tbsp	extra virgin olive oil
2	eggs, well beaten
½ cup	(125 mL) finely chopped fresh herbs (basil, oregano, tarragon, parsley)

Heat an omelette or nonstick pan on medium. Add the oil and heat for 1 minute. Add the beaten eggs. Let cook up to 1 more minute, until eggs start to set. Gently push edges of omelette into the centre of the pan, letting the liquid egg flow underneath the set egg until the entire mixture has begun to set and there is no liquid left in the pan. It should look like an egg "pancake." Gently flip the omelette over and sprinkle with the herbs. Fold the omelette in half and slide onto a warmed plate.

Makes 1 serving.

Eggs

Eggs are a staple in any kitchen. The best-tasting always come from someone who raises their own chickens. In Vancouver, as in many major cities, it is now legal to raise chickens in our own backyards. Not up for that yet? Then look for the following labels when purchasing eggs:

- Certified organic: chickens live cage free, have access to the outdoors, are audited for animal welfare

- Free range: cage free, access to outdoors, not audited

- Free run: cage free, not audited

- All other eggs come from caged birds.

Roast Pork Florentine

In Florence, when you ask your butcher for the arrosto *(which means roast in Italian), he'll know what to give you. We prefer to make our own version with garlic and rosemary stuffing, but you can use your imagination to create the filling for this roast. We like to serve it with a Cumberland sauce, but any fruity accompaniment is good. (Note: You will need a meat thermometer for this recipe, as well as twine for tying the roast.)*

¼ cup	(60 mL) extra virgin olive oil
6	garlic cloves, finely chopped
2 tbsp	coarsely chopped rosemary leaves and sprigs
1 tbsp	salt
1 tbsp	freshly ground black pepper
3–5 lb	(1.5–2.2 kg) rolled boneless pork loin roast

Preheat oven to 375°F (190°C).

Using a food processor or mortar and pestle, combine the olive oil, garlic, rosemary, salt, and pepper to form a coarse paste.

Unroll the pork and pat dry with a paper towel. Spread half the paste over the meat. Roll up the pork lengthwise like a jellyroll and tie every 2 in (5 cm) with twine. Using a sharp knife, make 1-in (2-cm) slits over top of the pork and stuff the remaining paste into the slits. Let stand at room temperature for 1 hour.

Place the pork in a large roasting pan and roast for 45 minutes, basting the meat occasionally. When internal temperature of the roast reaches 160°F (71°C), remove from oven and let stand for 10 minutes, then carve and serve with Cumberland sauce (recipe follows).

Makes 6–8 servings.

Cumberland Sauce

An old English recipe to complement the "Italian" port roast. Perfect!

1	(250 mL) cup red current jelly
1 tbsp	orange zest
1 tbsp	lemon zest
1 tsp	grated fresh ginger
1 tsp	dry mustard
½ cup	(125 mL) port
2 tbsp	orange juice
1 tbsp	lemon juice

In a small saucepan, warm the jelly. Add the orange and lemon zests and ginger. Mix the mustard with the port and add to the jelly mixture. Add the orange and lemon juices and simmer for 10 minutes.

Makes 1½ cups (375 mL).

Barbecued Lamb

Lamb has always been a mainstay in Vancouver. Early British residents brought the roast-lamb-with-mint-jelly Sunday-dinner tradition when they arrived, and the strong community of Greek residents from Vancouver's west side taught us all to love Greek-style barbecued lamb.

The shoulder roast has more fat than the leg cut and tastes richer, but the cooking method, below, is the same for both.

4–6 pound	(1.8–2.7 kg) lamb shoulder roast or 12 small lamb shoulder or loin chops
	salt and freshly ground pepper, to taste
3	lemons, juiced, then cut into 2-in (5-cm) pieces
3 tbsp	dried oregano
6	garlic cloves, smashed
¾ cup	(225 mL) extra virgin olive oil

Season the lamb with salt and pepper. Combine the lamb with the rest of the ingredients in a sturdy plastic bag. Place the bag in a bowl and marinate in the refrigerator for 24 hours or up to 3 days (the longer it marinates, the better it tastes.) Turn meat over every 8 hours.

When ready to cook, remove from the bag and place lamb on a hot barbecue. Turn often while roasting until the skin is crisp and the meat is done, about 1 hour for the roast or 20 minutes for the chops.

Makes 4 servings.

Fruits, Sweets, & Baked Goods

Monica's Lemon Sponge Cake

After the richer sweets of winter, you'll enjoy this light lemony pudding cake, which can be served warm or cold. It has a soufflé-like quality but is easy to make. Serve with Judie's Rhubarb Sauce (opposite). Monica McLeod is Fiona's mom and a friend of Judie's.

3 tbsp	butter, softened	⅓ cup	(80 mL) fresh-squeezed lemon juice	
1 cup	(250 mL) white sugar	2 tsp	lemon zest	
4	egg yolks	1 cup	(250 mL) milk	
3 tbsp	all-purpose flour	4	egg whites	
¼ tsp	salt			

Preheat oven to 300° F (150°C).

In a large bowl, use an electric mixer to cream together the butter and sugar until well blended. Add the egg yolks and beat until light in colour and fluffy. Stir in the flour, salt, lemon juice, and zest. Gradually add the milk. Beat the egg whites until stiff and carefully fold into the batter. Pour into a shallow 1-qt (1-L) baking dish and set into a pan of hot water that comes half way up the sides of the baking dish.

Bake for 40 minutes, then increase heat to 350°F (180°C) and bake for another 5 minutes. A toothpick inserted into the centre of the cake should come out clean.

Makes 4–6 servings.

Lemons

Almost all commercial lemons in North America come from California and Arizona. Because they are harvested year round and store well, they are always available at the Market. A good lemon should have a smooth, thin rind and feel heavy for its size. The colour should be bright yellow; greenish lemons will be more acidic and less flavourful.

Keep your lemons at room temperature and roll them before squeezing for maximum juice yield. You can use lemons to acidulate water (2 tbsp lemon juice or vinegar to 4 cups [1 L] water): immersing delicate fruits and vegetables in this liquid will prevent greying or loss of colour. Alternately, you can simply sprinkle them with pure lemon juice.

Rhubarb Sauce

This is Judie's favourite sweet offering using the first fruit of the season. It's excellent on Monica's Lemon Sponge Cake (opposite), oatmeal, ice cream, yogurt, or on its own. Prepare this in a heavy saucepan and watch it closely as it will burn quickly. When picking or buying rhubarb, look for heavy stalks with shiny skin.

2 cups	(450 mL) rhubarb, cut into 1-in (2.5-cm) pieces
¼ tsp	salt
½ cup	(125 mL) sugar
2 tbsp	butter

In a heavy saucepan, combine the rhubarb with 1/4 cup (60 mL) water and salt. Add the sugar and mix until combined. Cook on low heat for 20 minutes. When the rhubarb is broken down, remove from the stove. When slightly cooled, stir in the butter until melted, this gives the rhubarb sauce a smooth, silky taste.

Makes 1 cup.

Sweet Things

Before the cupcake girls, there was the fudge lady. Linda Ashley of Old World Fudge has sold fudge and brought it to every Market-vendor gathering from the start. At the Old World store, you can see fudge being made and hear the bell ring when it's time to pour the fudge into the long mold to cool. Chocolate-nut has long been the favourite flavour. Linda is now serving the grandkids of her early customers.

Lemon and Pine Nut Shortbread

From the original edition. Shortbread is usually a holiday cookie; the addition of lemons and pine nuts in this recipe adds even more cheer.

½ cup	(125 mL) pine nuts, toasted
1 cup	(250 mL) unsalted butter, room temperature
½ cup	(125 mL) white sugar
2 tbsp	grated lemon rinds (from 2 lemons)
¼ tsp	salt
1¾ cup	(415 mL) + ¼ cup (60 mL) all-purpose flour, divided

Preheat oven to 300°F (180°C).

Crush the toasted pine nuts with a rolling pin or chop in a food processor until finely ground. Set aside.

In a large mixing bowl, cream the butter until soft and fluffy. Gradually add the sugar to the butter and mix well. Add the pine nuts, lemon rinds, and salt and mix well. Add 1¾ cup flour.

Turn the mixture onto a rolling board. Work the extra ¼ cup flour into the dough, as necessary, until the dough cracks. Pat or roll the dough to ½-in (1-cm) thickness. Cut into desired shapes with a knife, round glass, or cookie cutter.

Place on an ungreased cookie sheet and bake for 30 minutes, until pale golden brown at the edges.

Makes 24 cookies.

Maple Syrup

Greg Gaddy at L.B. Maple Treat.

Maple syrup from Quebec is truly the best in the world. Luc Bergeron and his company L.B. Maple Treat have had a shop in the Market since the 1980s, and the demand for his maple products has expanded worldwide. Luc and his partner June sponsored a sugaring-off weekend in the Market's back courtyard every spring throughout the 1990s. Sugaring off, the process of tapping sugar maples and boiling their sap to make syrup, runs for six weeks, beginning in March. The taste of maple syrup has long been understood to be a matter of timing: as the season progresses, the syrup gets darker and more intensely flavoured, mainly because of micro-organisms that develop in the sap as the weather gets warmer.

In Canada, different grades—called No. 1 (the lightest), No. 2, and No. 3 (the darkest)—are tapped at different points in the season. The No. 1 grade, the one usually available to consumers, is further divided into Extra Light, Light, and Medium.

Only sugar maples and grey maples are tapped for syrup in Quebec. Their trunks must reach 8 in (20 cm) in diameter before they can be tapped; this can take about forty-five years. The trees can live to be over 200 years old. Scientists are only beginning to work out how characteristics of soil and climate ultimately express themselves in the complex flavour of maple syrup.

Looking for local maple syrup at the Granville Island Market? Producers on Vancouver Island are just beginning to tap trees called big leaf maples. ***Bonne chance!***

Pouding Chômeur (Rustic Maple Syrup Pudding Cake)

This country-style pudding is often served in Quebec.

SAUCE:

1½ cups	(375 mL)	maple syrup
¾ cup	(180 mL)	water
2 tsp	(10 mL)	butter

BATTER:

1 cup	(250 mL)	flour
1½ tsp		baking powder
½ tsp		salt
1½ cup	(375 mL)	sugar
1 tbsp		butter
1		egg, beaten
⅓ cup	(80 mL)	milk

Preheat oven to 350°F (180°C).

Grease a 9-in square (2.5 L) or round (1.5 L) baking pan.

To prepare the sauce: In a saucepan, mix the syrup and water. Bring to a boil, remove from heat, add the butter, and set aside.

Use two bowls to prepare the batter. In the first, mix the flour, baking powder, and salt. In the second, cream the sugar and butter. Add beaten egg and mix well. Add dry ingredients, alternating with the milk, and combine until well mixed.

Spoon the batter into the prepared pan. Carefully pour sauce over batter. Bake for about 35 minutes, until cake is golden. Let cool before serving.

Makes 6 servings.

Maple Syrup Crème Brûlée

Crème brûlée is always a hit at dinner parties; this version is enhanced by the addition of maple syrup.

2 cups	(500 mL) whipping (heavy) cream
½	seeded vanilla bean or 1 tsp vanilla extract
1	egg
3	egg yolks
½ cup	maple syrup
6 tbsp	sugar

Preheat oven to 325°F (160°C).

In a medium heavy-bottomed saucepan on medium heat, warm the cream. Add the seeded vanilla bean or extract. Scald the cream; small bubbles will form at the edges of the pan.

In a large mixing bowl, whisk the whole egg, egg yolks, and syrup together. Add the scalded cream slowly into the egg mixture and whisk until smooth. Strain the mixture into a large measuring cup. Place 6 4-oz (120-mL) ramekins in a large roasting pan and fill each one half full with the egg mixture. Pour hot tap water into the pan so it reaches halfway up the sides of the ramekins.

Bake for 40 minutes or until the mixture sets to "wiggly stage" in the ramekins (there shouldn't be any liquid under the skin). Cool on a rack for 30 minutes, then refrigerate for at least 2 hours.

Preheat the broiler. Evenly sprinkle 1 tbsp sugar over each serving. Place ramekins on a cookie sheet and slide under broiler until sugar is caramelized. Watch carefully—they should be lightly browned. If you own a kitchen blowtorch, you can torch the tops until they are browned. Be careful not to burn yourself!

Serve immediately.

Makes 6 servings.

Traditional Cottage Cheese Cake

This easy-to-make dish is neither too rich nor too sweet. It is similar to a light, very moist cheesecake. Try making it with homemade cottage cheese (p. 109). Serve with fresh fruit or rhubarb sauce (p. 133).

2 cups	(500 mL) cottage cheese
1 tbsp	lemon rind
1 tsp	nutmeg
¼ cup	(125 mL) melted butter
⅓ cup	(80 mL) cream cheese
2 tbsp	lemon juice
1 tsp	vanilla
⅓ cup	(80 mL) granulated sugar
½ cup	(125 mL) all-purpose flour
½ tsp	baking powder
3	eggs

Preheat oven to 350°F (180°C).

Line an 8-in (20-cm) square pan with parchment paper.

Place all the ingredients in a large bowl and beat until well-mixed. Pour into prepared pan and bake for 50 minutes or until a toothpick inserted in the centre of the cake comes out clean. Let stand in pan for 10 minutes, then turn out, peel off parchment paper, and invert onto rack to cool.

Makes 10 servings.

Summer

The aisles are jammed and the courtyard is full. Customers jostle one another—looking, pointing, stopping to take pictures. Summer is the peak season at the Market as locals take advantage of warm weather and the tourists crowd in by bus and water taxi. There's a full array of gorgeous fresh produce, every shop is bustling, and each merchant strives to keep up with the demands of the busiest time of the year. The Market feels like a music festival as the buskers and performers bask in the attention of their appreciative audiences. The courtyard is packed with people picnicking on local produce, cheese, and bakery goodies or enjoying the readymade fare available from the diverse ethnic and local food stands.

On sunny summer weekends, the days start early and end late; the regulars often come early to beat the rush, and at the end of the day people stock up for their evening barbecues. Despite the frequent chaos, the Market in summertime is a beautiful thing to behold.

Appetizers & Snacks

Herb and Cheese Yogurt

Greek-style yogurt flavoured with fresh herbs is an easy-to-make appetizer. The grated Parmesan adds a savoury dimension to the tangy yogurt. This is great with crudités, crackers, or bread.

2 tbsp	minced fresh Italian parsley
2 tbsp	minced fresh marjoram leaves
1 tbsp	minced fresh chives
1 tbsp	minced fresh basil
1 tbsp	minced fresh chervil
1 small	garlic clove (optional), finely chopped
1 cup	(250 mL) Greek-style yogurt
½ cup	(125 mL) freshly grated Parmesan cheese
	freshly ground pepper, to taste

Chop all the fresh herbs and in a bowl, combine with the yogurt. Mix in the Parmesan cheese. Cover with wrap and refrigerate until serving. Season with pepper before serving.

Makes about 1 cup.

Hot and Spicy Olives

In the 1980s, we were just beginning to discover different types of olives. We've come so far from those tasteless, pitted canned black olives of our youth! For a milder taste, mix cracked green olives with toasted fennel seeds and olive oil.

3 tbsp	coriander seeds
1 tbsp	crushed dried chilies
1 tbsp	chopped garlic
4 cups	(1 L) cracked green olives
2 tbsp	finely chopped fresh parsley or coriander
1 cup	(250 mL) extra virgin olive oil
3–4	whole dried chilies

Grind the coriander seeds with a mortar and pestle or in a food processor. Add the crushed chilies and garlic. In a serving bowl, mix the spices with the olives, add the parsley and olive oil, and mix again. Marinate for at least 1 hour. Garnish olives with whole chilies.

Makes 4 cups.

Salad Rolls with Dipping Sauce

These Vietnamese-style rolls have stood the test of time in the Market. From the start, they were a dream item for our business, Fraser Valley Produce. This is a fresh, healthy fast food snack—not fried, not full of fat—an ethnic specialty that has become almost as popular as sushi. Our staff introduced it to us and helped make salad rolls a huge bestseller. Cảm ơn bọn.

½ lb	(250g) rice vermicelli
8 sheets	rice paper
½ lb	(250g) cooked chicken or shrimp
4	green leaf lettuce leaves
8	green onions, white section removed

In a large bowl, pour boiling water over the vermicelli to cover, stirring gently to separate strands. Soak for 5 minutes until soft. Drain and let cool.

Wet the rice paper with warm water by spraying, briefly soaking, or brushing with a pastry brush. Set dampened sheets on a tea towel. At one end of each sheet, arrange a row of chicken meat or shrimp. Lay half a leaf of lettuce on top (break it up, if you like). Arrange a small handful of vermicelli on the lettuce, and then 1 green onion on the vermicelli. Roll each round lengthwise, tucking in the ends as you go. The roll should be tight. A small piece of dampened rice paper laid over the filling makes the rolling easier. Cover finished rolls with a damp lettuce leaf until all are complete, and keep cool and moist until serving. Serve with Dipping Sauce (opposite).

Makes 8 salad rolls.

DIPPING SAUCE:

1 tbsp	canola oil
½ medium	onion, finely chopped
½ in	(1 cm) finely chopped fresh ginger
1 cup	(250 mL) hoisin sauce
½ cup	(125 mL) water
¼ cup	(60 mL) unsalted roasted peanuts, crushed

In a medium skillet on medium heat, sauté the onions in oil until golden. Add the ginger and stir briefly. Add the hoisin sauce and water. Reduce heat and simmer for 15 minutes, then let cool to allow sauce to thicken. Stir in the peanuts just before serving.

Makes 1½ cups.

A Good-Luck Omen

On opening day of the Market in July 1979, a young woman wearing a bikini walked off a sailboat moored at the back of the Market and came to Judie and Fred's stall. She paid for a single green pepper (then worth thirty-five cents) with a fifty-dollar bill. This was probably a good-luck omen, but right then they learned that one of the ongoing challenges of any retail business—and this was before there were loonies, toonies (one- and two-dollar coins), and debit cards—is finding enough change.

Duso's Pesto

The first recipe for pesto appeared in the American magazine Sunset *in 1946, but it didn't become popular in North America until the 1980s. Once again, we were there at the flowering of the fresh food revolution at the Granville Island Public Market when Duso's pesto became the new mayonnaise: good on everything. Note: If you want to make a larger batch, simply increase the amounts of each ingredient accordingly.*

2	garlic cloves
¼ cup	(60 mL) pine nuts
¼ tsp	salt
1 cup	(125 mL) fresh basil leaves, stems removed
½ cup	(125 mL) extra virgin olive oil
½ cup	(125 mL) freshly grated Parmesan cheese

This is best prepared in a food processor. Using a metal blade, pulse the garlic, pine nuts, and salt for a few seconds. Add the basil and blend briefly. Add the olive oil and blend again. When all ingredients are well-blended, scrape the pesto into a bowl and mix in the cheese.

If you plan to freeze the pesto, prepare as directed, but do not add the cheese. Freeze in plastic containers. Before using, thaw completely and mix in the cheese.

Makes 1 cup.

Mauro Duso.

Pesto variations

- Toast the pine nuts before preparing pesto to accentuate the nutty flavour

- Substitute walnuts or sunflower seeds for the pine nuts

- Add 2 tbsp freshly grated Romano Pecorino cheese with the Parmesan. Romano is saltier than Parmesan, so reduce or omit the salt

- Give the pesto a smoother flavour by adding 2 tbsp softened butter when you add the cheese. Or add the same amount of cooked potato, which makes it smooth without adding more fat

Serving suggestions:

- Spread on top of hard-boiled eggs sliced in half

- Toss with butter and boiled small potatoes

- Place a dollop in serving bowls of fish soup or minestrone

- Toss with hot cooked rice and grated mozzarella cheese

- Make pesto butter by blending 1 part pesto with 3 parts butter. Serve it with baked or broiled halibut steaks, broiled tomatoes, or French bread (a lively change from garlic bread)

Pasta with Pesto

Cook 1 lb (500 g) fresh fettuccine or angel hair pasta in boiling salted water until tender but firm (al dente), and drain. Toss quickly with 1 cup (250 mL) pesto and serve.

Makes 4–6 servings.

Pesto Vinaigrette

Blend 6 tbsp pesto with ⅓ cup (80 mL) wine vinegar and ⅔ cup (160 mL) olive oil. Drizzle over thin slices of ripe tomatoes and mozzarella cheese, or use as a dressing for potato and pasta salads.

Makes 1½ cups.

Soups & Salads

Gazpacho

This lovely, piquant Spanish soup was wildly popular in the 1980s—and it's still a favourite with us. Because it's served cold, it is perfectly refreshing on a warm summer's evening.

6	plum tomatoes, coarsely chopped
2	red bell peppers, seeded and coarsely chopped
1	English cucumber, coarsely chopped
1 small	red onion, coarsely chopped
¼ cup	(60 mL) white wine vinegar
¼ cup	(60 mL) extra virgin olive oil
3 cups	(750 mL) tomato juice
1 tbsp	lemon juice
1–2 tbsp	finely chopped fresh cilantro
1–2 drops	of your favourite hot sauce
1 tsp	Worcestershire sauce
	salt and freshly ground pepper, to taste
	croutons, chives, or parsley to garnish

In a food processor or blender, process the tomatoes, red peppers, cucumber, and red onions separately until they are finely chopped but not puréed. Place the vegetables in a large bowl and add the remaining ingredients. Garnish with croutons or herbs as desired.

Makes 8 servings.

Salad Dressing for Summer Greens

This light dressing keeps well in the refrigerator and is perfect for simple salads of mixed greens from the Market. Lettuce has come a long way—you can get a remarkable variety of fresh and organic lettuces to mix and match to your tastes and menu: arugula, endive, red and green leaf lettuce, mache, radicchio, mustard greens … the list goes on and on.

¼ cup	(60 mL) flax seed oil
¼ cup	(60 mL) apple cider vinegar
2 tbsp	maple syrup
1 tsp	freshly ground pepper

Place all the ingredients into a pint jar with a tight lid and shake well. Store in the refrigerator and shake well before using.

Makes ¾ cup.

Judie's Potato Salad

Russets are no longer the only potato; they're now readily available in different shapes, sizes, colours, and flavours. The best news was the introduction of Yukon Golds in the late '80s. Developed in Canada, it has become the new all-purpose potato, known for its firm texture and natural buttery flavour and perfect for potato salads. This recipe is an old standby that still has legs. Judie served it for years at her juice bar, and it is well-loved by young and old.

5 lb	(2.2 kg) Yukon Gold potatoes, quartered, skins on
¼ cup	(60 mL) salt
2 cups	(500 mL) chopped celery
1 cup	(250 mL) chopped green onions, including tops
1 cup	(250 mL) sliced radishes
4–6	hard-boiled eggs, chopped

DRESSING:

1½ cup	(375 mL) good quality mayonnaise
1½ cup	(375 mL) sour cream
¼ cup	(60 mL) juice from sweet pickles (or to taste)
	salt and freshly ground pepper, to taste

In a large pot of salted water, boil the potatoes until soft. In a large mixing bowl, combine the celery, green onions, radishes, and eggs. In another bowl, combine the dressing ingredients. (More pickle juice means a moister potato salad.)

Let the potatoes cool, then chop into bite-sized pieces. Season with salt and pepper and mix with the other ingredients in the large bowl. Add dressing, and toss lightly and quickly so potatoes don't get mashed. Cover and refrigerate for at least 3 hours (overnight is even better).

Makes 6–8 servings.

Tuscan Bean Salad

Perfect as a side-dish at a barbecue or picnic lunch. Add 1 small tin of tuna or ½ cup (125 mL) cubed mozzarella cheese for extra protein to make it a meal in itself, and take it to work for a lunch-time treat.

1½ cups	(375 mL) dried white navy beans or 2 14-oz (398-mL) cans cooked white beans
½ medium	red onion, finely chopped
½	red bell pepper, finely chopped
½	yellow bell pepper, finely chopped
½ cup	(125 mL) sun-dried tomatoes, coarsely chopped

DRESSING:

¾ cup	(185 mL) extra virgin olive oil
½ cup	(125 mL) red wine vinegar
1 tsp	Dijon mustard
2 tbsp	finely chopped fresh oregano or basil
½ tsp	salt
	freshly ground pepper, to taste

If using dried beans, cover them with water and soak overnight. Drain and rinse. Place the beans in a medium saucepan of water and bring to a boil. Reduce the heat and simmer for 50 minutes or until the beans are tender. Drain the beans and rinse with cool water, then let cool.

In a medium mixing bowl, combine the cooked or canned beans, onion, peppers, and tomatoes. In a jar or small bowl, combine the dressing ingredients and mix well. Pour the dressing over the bean salad, mix well, and refrigerate for at least 1 hour before serving.

Makes 4 servings.

Vietnamese Chicken Salad

Coleslaw is a familiar salad that's usually made with cabbage, carrots, and other sturdy vegetables, and sometimes nuts or seeds. The dressing can be creamy and sweet or clear and tart. Granville Island's Stock Market has a horseradish-based dip as well as a lime-infused dressing that is delicious on coleslaws. This Asian version, from the folks at Fraser Valley Juice on Granville Island, includes chicken, fish sauce, and tart grapefruit.

While most coleslaws get better after the flavours marry for at least several hours, this one is better when served fresh.

1	boneless, skinless chicken breast (about 6 oz/170g), cooked
3 cups	(750 mL) thinly sliced green cabbage
3	carrots, cut into 1-in (2.5-cm) slices
½ cup	(125 mL) diced onion
½ cup	(125 mL) chopped celery
½ cup	(125 mL) finely chopped mint
½ cup	(125 mL) finely chopped cilantro
½	grapefruit, divided into sections

DRESSING:

½ cup	(125 mL) fish sauce
2	cloves garlic, chopped
¼ cup	(60 mL) sugar
	hot sauce, to taste
½ cup	(125 mL) water

Slice the chicken into bite-sized pieces and set aside. In a large salad bowl, combine the cabbage, carrots, onions, celery, and herbs. Mix all the dressing ingredients in another bowl. Add the chicken and dressing and mix well. Top with grapefruit and serve immediately.

Makes 8 servings.

Seafood Pasta Salad

This classic recipe is from the first edition. Back then, we wrote, "The secret to its taste is the tangy marinade, which is absorbed by the pasta before dressing is added." It makes a great summer lunch or light dinner.

½ lb	(250 g) dried rotini (spinach or tri-colour pasta is a nice touch)

MARINADE:

¼ cup	(60 mL) red wine vinegar
3 tbsp	lemon juice
2 tsp	finely chopped fresh basil
1	garlic clove, finely chopped
1	dried chili pepper, crumbled

DRESSING:

½ cup	(125 mL) mayonnaise
½ cup	(125 mL) cream cheese
¼ cup	(60 mL) wine vinegar
½ tsp	Dijon mustard
2 tsp	finely chopped fresh dill
1 tbsp	lemon juice

1 cup	(250 mL) shrimp, crab, or any combination of cooked fish
	chopped fresh dill, to garnish

Cook the pasta in boiling water until al dente (8–10 minutes), then drain and place in a large bowl.

In a small bowl, combine the red wine vinegar, lemon juice, basil, garlic, and chili and pour over the hot pasta.

Let the pasta cool in the marinade and then refrigerate until chilled. Drain excess liquid after cooling. In a bowl, combine the dressing ingredients and toss with the pasta to mix well. Keep in the refrigerator if not serving immediately. Mix in the seafood just before serving. Garnish with fresh dill.

Makes 4 servings.

Vegetables

Summer Baked Beans

We love baked beans, but in the summertime it's too hot to have the oven on for the hours required to cook them. One summer, we did the whole pork, molasses, and brown-sugar routine, put it in a low-heat oven, and forgot about it—that is, until coming home late to find the house smelling like a backyard cookout. That's when we remembered this recipe. You've probably seen lima beans in tomato sauce in deli cases. This is the homemade version. It's meatless and can be done on top of the stove or in the oven. It's always better the day after making it—usually the case with anything cooked in tomato sauce. (And, yes, technically beans aren't a veggie, but a legume.)

½ cup	(125 mL) diced onions
1 cup	(250 mL) diced carrots
¼ cup	(60 mL) extra virgin olive oil
2 cups	(500 mL) dried lima beans, soaked overnight
2 tbsp	chopped fresh dill
2 cups	(500 mL) good quality tomato sauce
	salt, to taste

Preheat oven to 350°F (180°C).

In a large pot on medium heat, sauté the onions and carrots in oil until soft. Mix in the drained beans and dill. Add the tomato sauce and salt. Cover and cook in the oven or on the stove top or for 45 minutes, checking moisture level and tenderness of the beans.

Makes 4 servings.

Pan-Bagnat

Although Vancouver's weather—even in the summer—doesn't evoke the feel of the south of France, this French-inspired sandwich, a simple variation on the flavours of a Niçoise salad, makes for a perfect summer picnic item, whether on the West Coast or elsewhere.

½	French baguette
1	garlic clove, halved
¼ cup	(60 mL) extra virgin olive oil
¼ cup	(60 mL) balsamic vinegar
1 6-oz	(175-g) can tuna (solid white albacore is best)
1 large	tomato, thinly sliced
1 very small	red onion, thinly sliced
2	hard boiled eggs, thinly sliced
¼ cup	(60 mL) pitted and finely chopped Niçoise or kalamata olives
4 slices	anchovy filets or 2 tsp anchovy paste
	salt and freshly ground pepper, to taste

Slice the baguette lengthwise and remove some of the soft bread from the centre to make a well. Rub the garlic clove over the surface to perfume it. In a small bowl, combine the oil and vinegar and brush liberally over both slices. Neatly arrange the rest of the ingredients on the bottom slice, then cover with the top. Press down firmly and tightly wrap in plastic wrap or parchment paper. Let sit at room temperature for about 2 hours. (If you prefer, you can refrigerate it for 2 hours.) Cut in half and serve.

Makes 2 servings.

Grilled Vegetables

These go beautifully with barbecued or grilled meats or fish. Don't worry if the veggies get a little blackened in the process, but keep an eye on them—they can burn quickly.

2	red bell peppers, cored and quartered
2	yellow bell peppers, cored and quartered
1 medium	red onion, quartered
1 head	fennel, upper stalks removed and quartered
2 large	carrots, cleaned and cut on an angle, about ½-in (1 cm) thick
2 large	parsnips, cleaned and cut on an angle, about ½-in (1-cm) thick
2 tbsp	extra virgin olive oil
2 tbsp	balsamic vinegar
	salt and freshly ground pepper, to taste

Preheat barbecue to high.

Place all the vegetables in a medium bowl and toss with the oil. Place the vegetables on the grill. You may want to use a basket or grill plate to prevent the veggies from falling through the grill onto the fire. Turn the veggies as they cook until they are browned and softened. Remove from grill and put back in the bowl. Toss with the balsamic vinegar and season with salt and pepper. Serve at any temperature.

Makes 4 servings (as a side).

Cheap Eats and Market Fast Foods

Granville Island Public Market has a longstanding policy of not allowing chain or corporate companies to do business on the island, which is perhaps most notable in the food stand section.

The Market offers a great variety of ready-to-eat snacks and meals from the culinary cultures of Greece, Mexico, India, China, Japan, Vietnam, Poland, Germany, and Italy. Fast food here has moved along with the times. First there was fish and chips; now there is sushi, crêpes, butter chicken, taco salads, sausage rolls, salad rolls, fruit pies, ice cream, salmon pies, pot pies, rice pudding, hot cereal, freshly made flour or corn tortillas, beans and rice, perogies, barbecue pork, pizza, and cabbage rolls. Be sure to visit the Market on an empty stomach!

Here are some take-away menu ideas for a quick and delicious dinner:

- Get your own tiffin and fill it with Indian comfort food: tandoori chicken kebobs, or masala chicken breasts

- Pick up some lasagna, already baked, and big Italian meatballs on a skewer that you can broil at home while making a salad

- Buy cooked sausages or cabbage rolls, and add some fresh crusty buns (all within reach of the west side of the Market)

- Get a spinach pie, buy a freshly made Greek salad, then pick up lamb kebobs or meatballs to grill at home

Grilling Fish

To guarantee succulent grilled fish, make the most of its naturally lean and tender qualities. Oil the surface of the grill before using. Handle the fish carefully, as the flesh is delicate. While grilling, baste frequently with a sauce that can be as basic as melted butter mixed with lemon juice. To test for doneness, use a fork to carefully push flakes apart at the thickest point. The fish should be opaque and the juices should run clear. Don't overcook the fish.

If you are cooking a whole fish and don't own a specially designed fish barbecue basket, make a foil "basket": Cut two pieces of heavy aluminum foil as long as the fish and about 2½ times as wide and stack for double thickness. Brush oil on the foil, then perforate with pencil-sized holes. Place on the grill, oiled side up. Place the whole fish slightly off centre on the foil. Halfway through cooking, close the foil over the fish, flip the package, and re-open to complete cooking. Brushing the fish with a good olive oil after removing from the grill enhances its flavour.

Janice and Alanna Kariotakas of the Salmon Shop.

Entrées

Grilled Salmon Two Ways

Perfect for impressing your guests, BC salmon (Coho, Sockeye, Pink, Chum, White and Pink Spring) is a wonderful way to showcase the fabulous local bounty that the Market has to offer. We kept this pair of recipes simple. You can add your favourite sauce (the pesto on p. 148 works beautifully!) to enhance the grilled salmon or garnish with just a wedge of lemon. Serve with roasted new potatoes and a simple salad.

OPTION 1:

1 whole	salmon fillet, about 2 lb (1 kg)
	salt and freshly ground pepper, to taste

Preheat barbecue to medium. Oil the grill to prevent sticking.

Place the fillet, skin side down, on the barbecue. Close the lid and let the salmon cook through, about 10–15 minutes. Platter and serve.

Makes 4 servings.

OPTION 2:

4 tbsp	mayonnaise (full fat is best)
1 tbsp	lemon juice
1 tsp	salt
1 tbsp	freshly ground pepper
1 whole	salmon fillet, about 2 lb (1 kg)

Preheat barbecue to medium. Oil the grill to prevent sticking.

In a small bowl, mix the mayonnaise, lemon juice, salt, and pepper. Place the fillet, skin side down, on a sheet of foil and evenly spread the mayonnaise mixture over top. Tent the foil over the salmon and place on barbecue. Grill for 10–15 minutes, until the fish is cooked through. Platter and serve.

Makes 4 servings.

Barbecued Ribs

To boil or not to boil? To rub or not to rub? However you like them, barbecued ribs are a huge treat during the summer. This recipe includes directions for pre-baking, which gives a guaranteed tender result (and, frankly, the idea of slow cooking on the barbecue can be a bit daunting). Use the barbecue to finish the cooking. Tip: *Bake the ribs the evening before so you don't overheat your kitchen on a summer day.*

2 racks	pork baby back ribs, about 1.5 lb (750 g), cut into 4-in (10-cm) pieces
1 tbsp	paprika
1 tbsp	onion powder
1 tbsp	garlic powder
1 tbsp	dry mustard
1 tsp	salt
1 tbsp	freshly ground pepper
	barbecue sauce (p. 172)

Preheat oven to 350°F (180°C).

Place the ribs on a baking sheet. Mix all the spices in a small bowl and rub into the ribs. Place the ribs in a roasting pan and bake for about 2–2½ hours. Let cool.

Preheat the barbecue to medium. Oil the grill to prevent sticking.

Slather ribs with sauce and place on the grill. Cook for about 15 minutes, until the outsides are slightly crispy and the ribs are warmed through. Brush them with more sauce while grilling.

Makes 6 servings.

Barbecue Sauce

For years we wouldn't have been caught with onion or garlic powder in our cupboard; now we love using these and other "old-time" spices for rubs and Southern-style sauces. This sauce is a combination of regional barbecue styles.

1 cup	(125 mL)	ketchup
1 cup	(125 mL)	chili sauce
⅓ cup	(80 mL)	brown sugar
¼ cup	(60 mL)	onions, minced
2 tbsp		garlic powder
2 tbsp		onion powder
1 tbsp		apple cider vinegar
1 tbsp		Worcestershire sauce
1 tsp		dry mustard
1–2 drops		your favourite hot sauce
		freshly ground pepper, to taste

In a medium saucepan on low heat, combine all the ingredients. Stir occasionally until the sugar has melted and the ingredients have blended well. Use immediately or cool and store in the refrigerator until ready to use.

Makes about 2½ cups.

Fruits, Sweets, & Baked Goods

Local Berries and Fruit Sweet and Tart

Early berries can be tart. By adding maple syrup, we sweeten them; by adding diced mango, we make them shine.

2 cups	raspberries
2 cups	blueberries
12 small	strawberries (if large, slice them)
1 large	mango (optional), diced
½ cup	(125 mL) maple syrup
3 tbsp	balsamic vinegar
	a few mint leaves for garnish

Rinse the raspberries and blueberries and drain well. Wash and hull strawberries and place in a salad bowl. Add the other berries and mango. In a small bowl, mix the maple syrup and balsamic vinegar. Combine with the fruit. Divide among 4 small serving bowls and garnish with mint leaves.

Makes 4 servings.

Are All Fruits Created Equal?

When talking produce, soft fruit doesn't mean ripe fruit; it's a term for a variety that needs a temperate climate and grows on trees or woody shrubs, such as kiwi and grapes. Small fruit usually means berries or bramble fruit. Stone fruits include peaches, plums, and apricots.

Confused about what's in season? Check out the signs on produce displays and look for what's local. But what about those times when you can't resist lychee just when local cherries become available, or mangoes when you should be buying local peaches? Relax; let your taste buds do the choosing.

Grilled Pineapple

Summertime is grilling time. Fruit on the barbecue is a new trick to us old-school cooks, but will make a nice addition to your grilling repertoire. Just remember to oil the grill beforehand.

½ medium	pineapple
1 tbsp	grated fresh ginger root
1 tbsp	light brown sugar

Cut the pineapple lengthwise into ½-in (1-cm) thick spears. Place pineapple, ginger, and brown sugar in a resealable plastic bag. Seal bag and allow pineapple to marinate for 5 minutes.

Place the pineapple spears on a preheated grill that has been sprayed or brushed with cooking oil. Grill until heated through, about 8 minutes, turning once. Remove to a serving platter, then cover with foil to keep warm.

Makes 4 servings.

The Pineapple Express

Here are a few tips about selecting a good fresh pineapple. Pull an inside leaf from the crown: it should detach easily. Even more importantly, check the colour of the shell: a greenish pineapple may be ripe, but a yellow to golden-orange he almost always means a beautiful amber fruit with a sweet taste. Use your sense of smell, too: a pineapple on sale could be starting to ferment, so your nose will let you know if it's a real bargain.

Roasted Figs

When we first arrived in Vancouver, we noticed many fig trees covered with netting or plastic. We finally asked a gardener about them one day and were given a lengthy explanation—in Italian. We later learned the netting protects the figs from birds that are savvy to the allure of these delightful fruits. Roasted figs can be served with almost everything from goat cheese to ice cream to roasted or barbecued meats.

12	fresh figs
2 tbsp	extra virgin olive oil
2 tbsp	honey or maple syrup
2 tbsp	port wine or liqueur
4	1-in (2.5-cm) strips of lemon peel

Preheat oven to 400°F (200°C).

Cut the stems off the figs and slice them in half lengthwise. Toss the figs with the rest of the ingredients in a medium baking dish. Cover with foil and bake for 15–20 minutes. Let cool.

Makes 4 servings.

Caramelized Apricots

Like our spring rhubarb sauce, this summer treat goes wonderfully with yogurt or ice cream and really revs up your morning oatmeal.

6	fresh apricots
2 tbsp	unsalted butter
2 tbsp	sugar

Slice the apricots in half and remove pits. In a skillet on medium heat, melt the butter and sprinkle in the sugar. Cook until sugar melts, about 2–3 minutes. Add the apricots, cut side down. Cook on medium-high heat until golden brown, about 3–5 minutes. Turn apricots over and cook the other side for 1–2 more minutes. Transfer to a plate, skin side up, to cool slightly. Slip off skins and discard.

Makes 3 servings.

A Smokin' Piece of Art

A smoke shop/newsstand is common to any market scene in Europe and Asia. Voula and Alex Garifaldis, originally from Greece, were owners of a corner store in Vancouver's Point Grey area, and they knew the Market was the place to be. They smoke and they know lots of people—so their smoke shop was a fixture from the start!

But in the 1990s, Vancouver became "smoke-free" and cigarettes, cigars, and smoking-related materials in shops had to be hidden from view. Voula and Alex had commissioned a student from the Emily Carr School of Art on Granville Island to paint a mural of a woman rolling cigars, as Voula had visited Cuba and wanted a piece of art that would recall her trip and reflect her business. The smoke police, as Voula called them, would have none of it, and insisted that the mural be covered.

"But it's art," Voula said, "and it doesn't encourage smoking."

"If it's art," said the smoke police, "it has to have a price tag on it."

But the Garifaldis won out. Although their smoke shop has since been sold, if you look high above the back counter, you can still see part of the mural—with no price tag.

Tiramisu in a Snap

An elegant and light ending to a barbecue meal, this is a quick version of the popular dessert.

1 cup	(250 mL) strong coffee or espresso
⅓ cup	(80 mL) amaretto liqueur or almond-flavoured syrup
12	ladyfinger biscuits broken into large chunks
1 cup	(250 mL) whipping cream
¼ cup	(60 mL) light brown sugar
½ cup	(125 mL) grated dark chocolate

In a medium bowl, mix the coffee and amaretto or almond syrup. Add the biscuit chunks and soak for no longer than 2 minutes or they will turn to mush.

In a large bowl, whip the cream and sugar together until it forms soft peaks.

Divide a portion of the biscuits among 4 dessert goblets or large wine glasses. Cover with a some of the whipped cream. Repeat layering biscuits and cream, twice to create 3 layers, ending with a layer of the whipped cream on top. Sprinkle with grated chocolate and serve.

Makes 4 servings.

Home Ripened Fruit

Many fresh fruits taste better and last longer if they are ripened at home and stored properly. Nectarines, peaches, pears, and plums usually need home ripening; leave them at room temperature. Most melons, if firm when purchased, can stand at room temperature until they start to soften slightly at the blossom end and develop a sweet, pleasant melon scent—then you'll want to eat them right away or refrigerate.

Tomatoes, unless they have been cut, should not be refrigerated. Stand them stem up on the kitchen counter, away from direct sunlight.

Some fruits should be ripe when purchased, including lemons, limes, oranges, tangerines, grapefruit, apples, grapes, pineapples, and cherries. Refrigerate for storage but let the fruit come to room temperature for the best taste.

Index

Carol Jensson (left) and Judie Glick (right) were among Granville Island's first merchants, Carol as owner of the Blue Parrot coffee bar and Judie as co-owner of the Fraser Valley Juice and Salad Bar. Carol is now a food stylist for Vancouver's film industry, while Judie (co-author of the original *Granville Island Market Cookbook*) has been writing about food since 1968.